Advanc
Opportu

"The authors of *Opportunity Knocking: How Community College Presidents Can Lead a New Era of Advancement* provide practical advice for both current and aspiring community college leaders, including useful information about fundraising, supporting an advancement office, building strong foundation boards, the use of social media for advancement, breaking down the barriers to public-private partnerships, engaging alumni and friends, marketing, and much more. All of us who are serious about making our colleges the best they can be should put this book at the top oof our reading lists."

George R. Boggs, President and CEO Emeritus of the American Association of Community Colleges and Superintendent/President Emeritus of Palomar College

---

"This collection of powerful ideas and practical experience and advice is highly relevant to today's challenges and opportunities. More important, it is about the definition of next-generation leadership! It builds on all that has been done with pride ... and takes the story, the impact and the success to a whole new level with confidence and conviction."

William D. Green, Former Chairman and CEO, Accenture

"Embracing advancement is not only a response to economic necessity, it also leads to dynamic and creative leadership in our nation's vital community colleges. This volume is a welcome compendium of philanthropic leadership lessons, based on demonstrated success, shared with others so they too can thrive."

Amir Pasic, Dean, Indiana University Lilly Family School of Philanthropy

---

"Community college leaders can use this publication as a much-needed playbook for advancing their institutions to thrive in the future. It gives the practical and actionable advice required for anyone who wants to lead a community college in the coming decades."

Jeffrey J. Selingo, Contributing Writer, *The Chronicle of Higher Education* and *The Washington Post,* Author, *College (Un)Bound: The Future of Higher Education and What It Means for Students*

Opportunity Knocking

Opportunity Knocking

How Community College Presidents Can Lead a New Era of Advancement

EDITED BY PAUL C. HEATON

WASHINGTON, D.C.

ISBN: 0–89964–453–8
ISBN 13: 978–0–89964–453–0
Printed in the United States of America

Library of Congress Cataloging-in-Publication Data

Opportunity knocking : how community college presidents can lead a new era of advancement / Edited by Paul Heaton.
pages cm
Includes bibliographical references and index.
ISBN 978-0-89964-453-0 (pbk. : alk. paper) -- ISBN 0-89964-453-8 (pbk. : alk. paper) 1. Community college presidents--United States. 2. Community colleges--United States--Administration.
LB2341.O68 2015
378.1'11--dc23

2015008987

Book design: O2 LAB · *o2lab.com*
Art Director: Angela Carpenter Gildner
Editorial Director: Doug Goldenberg-Hart

CASE
1307 New York Avenue, NW
Suite 1000
Washington, DC 20005–4701

CASE Europe
3rd Floor, Paxton House
30 Artillery Lane
London E1 7LS
United Kingdom

www.case.org

CASE Asia-Pacific
Unit 05–03
Shaw Foundation
Alumni House
11 Kent Ridge Drive
Singapore 119244

CASE América Latina
Berlín 18 4to piso, Colonia Juárez
Código Postal 06600, México D.F.
Delegación Cuauhtémoc
México

CONTENTS

SECTION III: FUNDRAISING

SECTION IV: COMMUNICATIONS & ENGAGEMENT

FOREWORD

A fresh, new look at advancement prospects and practices at community colleges could not be more timely. In fact, time *and* money are and will continue to be overriding concerns for college leaders into the foreseeable future. The key questions are how much time should be allocated to advancement during each leader's time-starved schedule, and how can financial resources be generated for a growing mission when the traditional funding model is so clearly broken?

Recalibrating the funding model does not—must not—dilute our core values: opportunity, equity and academic excellence. But as the American Association of Community Colleges (AACC) 2012 report from the 21st-Century Commission on the Future of Community Colleges states emphatically, "virtually everything else must change." Smarter, strategic and more aggressive advancement efforts to sustain our values and transform our institutions simply must be a top priority for every leader.

The forces driving the need for enhanced and more diverse funding mechanisms have been well documented: declining enrollments after years of record growth, fewer tuition dollars compounded by decreased state funding, long-delayed infrastructure maintenance and needed expansion, and demands to increase student completion rates and amp up accountability measures. These and other factors have irreparably destabilized the traditional community college funding model. As Maricopa Community Colleges chancellor Rufus Glasper noted in a recent *Community College Daily* commentary, "We need to stop looking to the past as a means to change our future."

AACC and its colleague organizations have been working to prepare the new kind of leader a new age demands—an innovative thinker who not only embraces the "big ideas" but also commits time and energy to bring them to fruition. The work of the 21st-Century Commission; the ambitious quest to develop an implementation guide for the commission's recommendations; and the creation of a perpetual, online resource center of ideas and best practices are aimed at advancing our institutions to better serve students and communities.

In putting together this practical and reality-based advancement primer, the Council for Advancement and Support of Education (CASE) has tapped some of our most insightful and experienced leaders, courageous innovators who have tackled head-on our thorniest issues. The ideas and lessons presented here are based on individual experiences, but they address common and persistent problems. With close to 75 percent of community college leaders expected to retire over the coming decade, this publication adds to a critical arsenal of resources and should be essential reading for aspiring campus leaders, as well as for those now on the job.

The issues presented in this new publication underscore, amplify and complement the work of AACC and others relating to transformational leadership and institutional advancement. Among myriad leadership challenges, chapter authors suggest ways to:

- define and enhance the CEO's role in fundraising, advocacy and communication;
- hire, support and evaluate top-notch development and marketing staff;
- establish successful and sustainable public-private partnerships;
- build infrastructure to grow endowments and capital campaigns;
- recruit and support effective foundation boards vis-à-vis boards of trustees;
- harness the power of alumni groups;
- leverage social media and other technologies; and
- get to the next, more rewarding level.

Community colleges can no longer be hesitant or half-hearted in pursuing the financial support they need and deserve. Although the colleges have been in operation for more than a century, far too many are still on the lower rungs of the advancement ladder. According to a 2013 survey conducted by the Council for Aid to Education, of a total $33.8 billion in contributions to higher education, only $212 million went to community colleges. And an analysis of the most recent IRS Form 990 data indicates that average assets held by community college foundations total a modest $5.6 million.

The sunny-side of that dismal equation is the broad opportunity it presents for improvement. Recent multimillion-dollar bequests to Broome Community College and others prove that the potential exists, especially when more wealth is being transferred than at any other time in our nation's history. Among other funding strategies, planned giving is key to larger gifts and more robust endowments. Yet recent analysis by the Wilmington Trust notes that only a third of community colleges mention so-called legacy societies on their websites and in marketing materials. We must do better—with informed leadership and a generously supported development function.

Community college leaders are not routinely exposed to advancement training during their career progression and often must learn on the job. That, too, is changing.

Events and resources provided by CASE and the Council for Resource Development, augmented by more targeted leadership programs, are helping current and would-be leaders acquire advancement skills or hone existing skills in new ways. *Opportunity Knocking: How Community College Presidents Can Lead a New Era of Advancement* reinforces proven principles of successful advancement practice.

Most important, developing college leaders as fundraisers-in-chief is about much more than raising money. As Mt. San Antonio College president Bill Scroggins writes in his chapter ("Getting to the Next Level: What Does It Take?"), the CEO's "vision for the foundation must incorporate today's reality, tomorrow's goal, and a path to connect the two."

It starts, as is so often the case, with the committed woman or man in the CEO mirror.

Walter G. Bumphus is president and CEO of the American Association of Community Colleges.

INTRODUCTION

Paul C. Heaton

It is a frightening statistic: Close to 75 percent of community college leaders are expected to retire in the next 10 years.

The traditional "pipeline" of future campus leaders simply does not have the capacity to provide the people needed to fill those shoes. Not only will there be a tsunami of new community college presidents in a few short years, but many of those presidents likely will not come from the halls of academe.

Regardless of where the next generation of leaders comes from, one thing is clear: Their colleges—and their ultimate success—will require more from their institutional advancement offices than ever before. Advancement goes far beyond fundraising; it represents the combined efforts and synergy of marketing, communications, alumni, government and corporate relations, as well as fundraising. Community colleges historically have managed to skimp by with minimal marketing, alumni relations and fundraising programs. Today they are paying the price, struggling to keep pace with the sea change in communications technology, competing to keep up with competitors' multimillion-dollar marketing campaigns and scurrying for large gifts to fill the void left by fewer public dollars—all while needing more funds to remain competitive in terms of programs, facilities and technology.

Far from being a dire situation, though, the next decade has the potential to be the most transformative period ever for community colleges.

With more people recognizing these institutions as local economic engines, agile and responsive to the learning needs of the community, their value and prestige will only grow. A new wave of leaders will have myriad opportunities to expand awareness of, interest in and public support for community colleges.

This publication is designed to help them do just that.

Whether you are a new president, or perhaps a sitting president who wants to expand your college's advancement efforts, this book offers sage advice from campus CEOs who have been where you are.

The book starts by tackling a fundamental question: Given all that presidents already have to do, why even bother with advancement?

The next three chapters provide guidance for the early months of a community college presidency, from a personal communications strategy to what to expect from your advancement staff.

Relationships with your foundation board, governing board and chief advancement officer will be central to your success, so three chapters address those dynamics.

Most community college presidents—as well as most human beings, I suspect—would say they do not like asking people for money. Chapter 9 debunks myths surrounding fundraising—what it is and what it is not—and helps you to see that you probably already have all the skills you need to be a successful fundraiser. You just may not realize it yet.

A comprehensive, successful advancement operation requires the campus leader to have vision and dedication, but there are many practical components as well. Chapters dive *into* specifics on these topics:

- Developing public-private partnerships,
- Pursuing major gifts,
- Investing in advancement,
- The importance of alumni relations,
- Social media,
- Crisis communications and
- Marketing and branding.

We conclude with advice useful for an advancement operation of any size or level of maturity: How do you take what you have and move it to the next level? It's a helpful conclusion and a reminder of what community college faculty instill in their students: We're all here to learn and grow, and that is a lifelong process.

You'll notice a common thread throughout these chapters: Presidents who are serious about advancement make it their job and the job of everyone on campus. This important work doesn't fall only to marketing staff or fundraisers. Successful advancement efforts ultimately are about building strong relationships—with and between faculty and staff, students, alumni, elected officials, media, community leaders, education partners, area business and industry, foundations and, of course, individual donors.

I was struck by this sentence in the bio of one of our many valued contributors: "He begins nearly every workday writing by hand a variety of cards, letters and other personal correspondence, which frames the day ahead for building and sustaining relationships and opportunities."

The work can be tedious, frustrating and time consuming, but if you follow the advice that the experienced authors of this book share, you will begin to discover energy and momentum that is infectious. It will elevate every aspect of your organization and provide some of the most memorable and rewarding aspects of your role as a campus leader.

Chapter 1

WHY BOTHER WITH ADVANCEMENT?

By William R. Crowe

The role of the community college president has changed dramatically over the past several decades. As our institutions have grown and matured, the presidency has become more complex and demanding. In more than 30 years of working in and around community colleges, I have never heard a president ask for more to do or complain that he or she had too much free time. As in my 15 years as president of Tyler Junior College (TJC) in Texas, you rarely have a dull moment.

But it is time for another fundamental change in the office of the community college president. This book is intended to explain why—and how—to accomplish that change.

For myriad reasons, community colleges have yet to fully embrace the notion of advancement—the alignment of fundraising, marketing, communications, alumni relations and public relations—to help them fulfill their missions and achieve their visions. Sure, there has been progress and some significant success, but growth and change in other areas have far outpaced those in advancement.

This book is a collection of stories and advice—from presidents to presidents (or aspiring presidents). Our hope is to inspire you and your colleagues to usher in a new era of advancement, setting in motion ideas and initiatives that will help your college today and, more important, position it—and you—for long-term success.

As with any significant change, there will be reluctance, setbacks and mistakes. Based on my experience, I can tell you that advancement work also can provide some of the most rewarding moments of your professional life. It can even be fun at times.

So let's get started.

There are three reasons for you to spend time developing and growing a vibrant advancement operation:

- It is in the long-term interest of your college.
- Significant philanthropic resources are available that will be given somewhere. Why not to your institution?
- It is in your long-term career and professional best interests.

Our colleges continue to be challenged with financial hardships. Over the past 30 years, state appropriations as a percentage of total revenue have fallen, on average, from 70 percent to 38 percent for community colleges. If you look at funding per contact hour or per student, the picture looks even worse. In addition, most colleges are under pressure to keep tuition and fees flat or at least to greatly reduce the rate of increases. And there is great pressure on those institutions with taxing authority to hold tax rates steady or even reduce tax levies.

All of these challenges are occurring at a time of rising operating costs, such as employee health care, combined with the challenge of dealing with aging campus infrastructures.

Add to this the need to create new academic programs, improve student success rates and add modern facilities and equipment, and the financial picture worsens even further. Institutions' long-term financial viability is at risk. Increasing enrollment as a way to boost the bottom line is no longer a sustainable model.

Advancement, including a robust fundraising operation, isn't a panacea, but it can go a long way toward closing the gap and providing not just resources but the momentum our colleges need. The short- and long-term health of your institution will improve if you build a solid advancement operation to support your efforts.

How much is at stake?

Philanthropy in the United States is a major source of revenue for education, religious organizations and other nonprofit groups, which collectively received more than $335 billion in 2013, according to Giving USA. Where does all of this money come from? Individuals account for nearly three-fourths of the total. That makes philanthropy a very personal action, one influenced by other individuals such as family, friends and even financial advisers. Because of the personally enriching nature of our work, and our community focus, community colleges are well positioned to cultivate individuals for private philanthropy.

Where is the money going? According to Giving USA, here is the breakdown:

Religious organizations	31%
Education	16%
Human services	12%
Gifts to foundations	11%
Health care	10%
Public-society benefit	7%
Arts, culture and humanities	5%

This list matters because, except for religious organizations, most community colleges play a significant role in every other charitable endeavor on the list. How much better positioned could our colleges be to match the interests of donors?

The annual Voluntary Support of Education (VSE) survey offers significant comparative data on the advancement efforts of colleges and universities. Although community college participation in the survey is low (around 19 percent), it is growing. You should encourage participation in the survey and use of VSE data to benchmark and improve performance.

According to the 2013 VSE survey, sources of private giving to public community colleges were broken down as follows:

Non-alumni individuals	35.5%
Corporations	26.4%
Foundations	25.2%
Other organizations	8.1%
Alumni	4.4%
Other	0.3%

Although the higher education numbers are a little different from the general philanthropy data, more than 40 percent of all gifts to community colleges still come from individuals.

As a faculty member at the University of Georgia, I have been conducting a longitudinal study of community colleges and their support foundations. My data come from more than 800 public community colleges and their support foundations. The key data in that study are funds raised per year and assets held in the foundation. Four years of data on all colleges have been collected so far and are available to interested institutions. Between this study, the VSE survey and Council for Advancement and Support of Education (CASE) surveys, ample data are increasingly available to you and your trustees.

Do you know how you stack up? As an example, for the most recent year with complete data, the average community college raised $803,465 and held in its foundation assets worth $5,578,894. When you compare your institution to others, there are many variables to consider (for example, maturity of the foundation, staff size), but you and your chief advancement officer should know where you stand, not just in terms of total numbers but in terms of the sources of funds, as well.

Take the long view

The average community college presidency now lasts only about five years. Although immediate and short-term needs must be addressed, you have been entrusted with your institution, and that includes ensuring its long-term sustainability. How do you want to be remembered? Whenever someone asked me what I wanted my legacy to be at TJC, I said, "I want the president 20 years from now to say he or she was so thankful that a certain program was put in place years ago." That future president doesn't have to remember my name, but I want him or her to know that someone in the past did something to help address current challenges.

Not only will you change the course of your institution, but you will also change the lives of many donors. Donors do not give just because of need. They want to give back to society and have an impact, and they believe that those with resources should help those without. As you develop relationships with donors and begin to make your case, don't talk about your needs and wants; talk about what you and donors might accomplish together.

Don't think about it as asking for money. You are giving donors an opportunity to make a difference. Oftentimes they will have tears in their eyes and become emotional when they make their gifts. It is a great feeling and so rewarding. I was working with a college recently that had just received its first $1 million gift. The president was so proud for both the institution and the donor. As he told his board about the gift, he said that the only thing the donor said to him when he handed him the check was "thank you." The donor thanked *him* for letting him support the college because he previously had not been aware of the opportunity. What a gift! My guess is there will be many gifts to follow. Can you imagine being thanked for accepting a $1 million check?

This is but one example of how your life will change for the better when you become involved in advancement. There also are pragmatic reasons for embracing advancement work.

Increasingly, experience in advancement is a job requirement in presidential searches, and fundraising accomplishments are included in annual presidential evaluations. It won't be long before advancement is a regular topic among members of the Association of Community College Trustees (ACCT), so expect more questions from your trustees. The good news is that their interest will provide support for you to increase resources for advancement. The bad news is that, if you are not actively engaged in advancement, you will face some challenging questions from your trustees.

In the past several years, there has been an increased emphasis on and awareness of community college advancement activities. CASE has opened a practice devoted solely to community colleges, conducting research, holding conferences and webinars, and publishing books such as this one. The work of CASE is going to shine a much brighter light on how well individual colleges are raising private funds. The Council for Resource Development (CRD) is another resource, singularly dedicated to community college fundraising. Both CASE and CRD are aggressively promoting professional development and best practices among community college CEOs, trustees and foundation boards.

Although there are many compelling reasons to embrace advancement, the reality is that you do not have a choice. Ongoing financial pressures, combined with demands for more resources, require a new revenue source for community colleges. Fortunately, we are well positioned to rapidly grow this increasingly vital aspect of our colleges. It won't be easy, but it will be among the most rewarding work you will do as president.

If you are anything like me, some of your best days as president are when you attend a student success ceremony. It could be commencement, a health science program pinning ceremony or a GED completion program—the places where you see tangible evidence of the work you do every day. Now imagine adding myriad other similar events to your days: attending donor thank-you lunches, opening a new lab, awarding new scholarships, celebrating employee and student gifts. Philanthropy can transform an institution ... and make for a joyful presidency in the process.

Top 10 principles for fundraising success

In the past six years I have been studying and working either directly or indirectly with every U .S. public community college and their support foundations. That experience, plus my time as president of Tyler Junior College (TJC), has helped me identify how we move advancement work forward in our colleges. Even colleges with the most sophisticated advancement operations need to get better.

There are many legitimate reasons why community colleges are behind. They have been largely the benefactor of robust state support. Our institutions also were in their formative years, when we struggled just to keep up with the growth. As young, new organizations in our communities, we enjoyed spectacular support at both the local and the state levels. The vast majority of our colleges are now entering maturity in the organizational life cycle, but they still have nascent advancement operations.

Community colleges today are in a position similar to where public universities were a few decades ago. Universities decided that private funding could help their institutions survive and grow, and they invested in people and resources. The results have been impressive and provide a glimpse of what is possible for community colleges ... if we are willing to invest in, and be systematic about, expanding our advancement operations.

Based on my experience, what follows are 10 principles that will help you regardless of where you and your institution are in advancement work. There are no simple solutions or "silver bullets." You will need persistence, patience, a plan and, occasionally, a thick skin. But above all, you have to act. As my spouse used to say when she was the chief operating officer of a national health care company, "Hope is not a strategy."

1. Hire experienced professionals

The number one challenge for us is to look at advancement as a profession that requires trained and experienced professionals. Because we are essentially community-based organizations, we tend to craft our advancement work much like the nonprofits in our communities.

Too many colleges I have encountered have hired a local "celebrity" to head up their advancement efforts. It could be the past chair of a United Way campaign, a retired public servant or anyone the college believed "knew everyone in town." It is helpful to have someone in place who knows the key players in town, but raising a significant number of dollars requires experience and a deep understanding of advancement well beyond personal contacts. There is no substitute for experience.

What if you inherited someone who is not the ideal chief advancement officer? It depends on how quickly you want to ramp up your fundraising efforts and success. If you believe your existing staff has potential and is trainable, get them professional development, but be clear about the reasons for doing so—and the goals.

There are many opportunities to receive training for both you and your staff. CASE provides regional and national conferences, and it has a vast library of books, white papers and other resources. CRD sponsors conferences and workshops for community college fundraisers and community college presidents. You can also employ consultants who will offer expert guidance. A good place to start would be to have a Peer Advancement Review performed by CASE or to engage an outside consultant to provide an assessment.

If you want to jump-start your advancement work, an experienced chief advancement officer can quickly assess your situation and devise a plan to move forward. He or she will also be able to assist in the professional development of your existing staff.

When I decided to get serious about our advancement work at TJC, I recruited two advancement professionals from private four-year institutions. Private institutions tend to have more development experience (and success) because they depend on fundraising for institutional survival. It turned out to be one of my best decisions as president. There were significant challenges (they often thought everything we did was from the dark ages), but they were able to move us along rapidly.

The real challenge was being able to support them and grow our efforts in a manageable way. But as the old saying goes, it is better to have to rein in an aggressive employee than it is to always have to push the employee to do more. The results were incredible! In a short period of time, we were engaged in a dynamic advancement environment, raising more funds than I would have imagined. We grew the Tyler Junior College Foundation into the sixth largest community college foundation in the United States, and it is consistently in the top 5 percent in funds raised annually.

It will serve you well in both the short and the long terms to make certain your advancement team is knowledgeable and well trained in all aspects of educational advancement and fundraising.

2. Enthusiastically embrace advancement

The number one complaint I hear when speaking to community college advancement professionals is that they cannot get their presidents engaged in their work. Although the demands on the presidency are great, your staff will not succeed without your wholehearted participation. There are some things that only the president can do. Setting the general direction for the college and allocating budget funds are two of them. There are also certain fundraising tasks that only you can do. You are likely already doing many of these but just need to put a little advancement "spin" on them.

Here are some tasks that served me well at TJC and that my research has reaffirmed:

- When speaking publicly, always include fundraising as part of your talk. Always! This doesn't mean you're asking for money at every step. Rather, talk about the impact of philanthropy and remind people of the many ways that they can support the college.
- Communicate to internal and external constituents about the college's needs, and how they can help achieve fundraising goals.
- Articulate to your governing board the needs of the college and the role private support should play. Encourage them to give to the college, although this can be a delicate matter, since they ultimately are in charge of the institution (i.e., your boss).
- Find ways to spend quality time with foundation board members, both as a group and individually. Your advancement staff has the primary responsibility for engaging the foundation board, but the members need to hear from the organizational leader.
- In many instances, you will be the "closer" in working with donors who are making large gifts.
- Get to know the planned giving and estate planners in your area. They direct a lot of giving and also influence the decisions donors make about where funds could be given.
- A few donors will simply want to work with the president. This may seem like a burden, but it is really a gift. As mentioned previously, you will find great satisfaction in helping to direct donors' gifts to places where they are happy and feel they are maximizing their gifts for good works.
- Develop an "elevator speech" for why donors should support your college. Mine was simple. I explained that there was no other place they could give their precious funds that would have a greater impact and maximize the value of their gifts than TJC. I often used the example of student scholarships and explained that with their gift we could serve three times as many students as a public university could (and 10 times as many as a private institution). Value and impact are important to donors.

- Find the right balance of time to spend doing advancement work. In some ways everything you do as president can have an advancement tie. If you have developed the right advancement staff, they will make great demands on your time. If you make donors a priority, they will make your college their priority.
- Enjoy the work and celebrate often. Your enjoyment will be evident to donors, prospects and your faculty and staff.
- Finally, get comfortable asking for money. The more you do it, the easier it will become, but you will need to do it. You have a lot to be proud of within your institution. Believe in it and yourself!

3. Identify institutional needs and priorities

Fundraising doesn't start with the solicitation. It starts with a need and a vision. You must set the agenda and communicate priorities for private philanthropy. Do you want to fund construction projects through a capital campaign? Raise endowed funds for student and/or faculty initiatives? Conduct an annual campaign to support a specific program? Raise undesignated money? You also must work in partnership with your advancement team to set short-, mid- and long-range fundraising goals.

Perform a thorough analysis of where your institution is, and where you want it to be. The outcome will help you determine staffing beyond the need for a seasoned chief development officer. If you are interested in immediate short-term results, then you might hire advancement staff to assist with annual funds and annual giving. If you already have a successful annual fund, you might want to focus on a capital campaign or an endowment campaign. There really is no one right way to build your advancement team. The organization should be a reflection of your strategy for giving. Ultimately, all of us would like to have it all: a robust annual campaign, successful comprehensive campaigns and a large endowment to support the college—all supported by a large advancement staff. The reality is that it takes time to get there.

At TJC we set off to build scholarship endowments for students and fund projects along the way. We never actually went into campaign mode. I told our advancement team that we were always in a campaign. When we would visit with donors we would just talk about what was going on and our immediate needs. In some ways I was being selfish, because I did not want our donors to think there was an end to our needs! Everything, though, was guided by our long-range goals and objectives. Of course, a donor sometimes had a special interest outside of our plan and we usually found a way to work that in and accept the gift. That said, sometimes you do have to say no to a gift if it truly does not match your needs or has too many strings attached.

4. Develop affinity groups

All of us have natural connections with students that we can use to build long-term affinity for the institution. Over the long term, nothing you do will have a larger impact on your college. Any program in which students and faculty spend extra time together is ripe for development. Health science programs which students complete in a cohort are a great example. If they are not in place already, form clubs and organizations around health science programs. The same can be said for most vocational and technical programs. The fine and performing arts programs are another area conducive to forming affinity groups. Co-curricular and extracurricular activities provide wonderful chances to build lasting and long-term connections between students and the institution.

One of the greatest opportunities is with Phi Theta Kappa (PTK). Make sure some of your best faculty members are involved as advisors in PTK and dedicate resources that allow your chapter to be active in state, regional and national meetings. You want your students to form strong connections with faculty, programs and the institution while they are enrolled.

The next step is to build an alumni association. Most of our institutions are old enough to have former students in prime giving stages of life. You have to keep them connected to the institution. At TJC we decided to really ramp up our alumni association. We started combing through records and trying to locate our former students. Founded in 1926, TJC had a fair number of former students but little information about where they were or what they were doing. The work of chasing down alumni can be difficult, but you can do it internally or with the help of an outside company.

Then you have to communicate with alumni, and engage them. Whenever I met with former students, I was always amazed at how they gushed about their experience. Those who transferred to finish a four-year degree usually said TJC was better than their university experience. Graduates of the technical and vocational programs would talk about specific faculty members who made a difference in their training and how well prepared they were to enter the workforce. Former student comments generally focused on a special faculty connection or the connection with a program or club. My guess is the majority of your former students feel the same way about your institution. Think about your students who transferred to and graduated from four-year institutions. How often do you think those institutions ask them to contribute? How often do they hear from you?

5. Think outside of your local community

Our mission is to meet the learning needs of the communities we serve. Most community colleges also tend to treat advancement as a purely local effort, hence, our propensity to hire the local celebrity as our chief advancement officer and for us to put in place fundraising programs like other nonprofits in the area. We tend to minimize the geographic reach of the impact we have as institutions.

I encourage you to think bigger. Some of your students stay in the area after completion, but take time to locate the others. You also provide trained workers to businesses that are global in nature and have offices around the world. For most of our work, being focused on the community is good. For your advancement work, though, you cannot ignore those who live outside of your service area. If you are not currently engaged with your former students, you will be amazed at what they are doing once you locate and reengage them. You will find success stories that put a spotlight not just on your alumni, but also on the quality education your college provides.

As we grew TJC's alumni association, we established chapters in every major city in Texas and in New York City and Los Angeles. We selected New York and Los Angeles because we had such a strong performing arts program, and as a result, many of our graduates went to those two cities. As president I would make an annual visit to each chapter to give a state of the college update and, of course, to talk about our fundraising efforts.

6. Events are not for fundraising

Many of our institutions rely on special events to raise funds. There are exceptions, but most events are not helping the bottom line as much as people think, because of the amount of staff time and resources they require. You would be much better off having the staff spend less time planning events and more time with individual donors and potential donors.

Events can serve a useful purpose, though. They are great for celebrating a special accomplishment, and they can also be useful for "friend-raising"—bringing individuals into the orbit of your institution. You might make some money from an event if it is primarily planned and operated by volunteers, but your time and energy for fundraising could be better spent elsewhere.

I encourage you to thoroughly review all of the special events at your college. Make sure there is a clear purpose beyond raising funds. If the primary purpose is to raise funds, have your financial team calculate the return on investment, including staff salaries and time required. I suspect that you will produce fewer and more targeted events as a result. This will make your advancement team happy—and more successful.

7. Every gift matters

Sometimes we get so involved in pursuing large gifts that we ignore the smaller donors. There is a pretty solid belief within the advancement profession that small gifts often lead to larger gifts. I do believe that, at times, a small gift can lead to a larger gift or, if handled correctly, to additional gifts. Even if that is not true, every gift is given to your institution with a certain level of trust. As president, you are the keeper of that trust. So honor all donors often. In my experience, even donors who say they do not like recognition really do. I have also found that donors like to have opportunities to be around other donors to the college. That may be a good reason to have a special event! You also want to find opportunities to visit with donors when you are not asking them for something. If the only time they see you or your advancement staff is when you are asking for a gift, chances are good the relationship will not last.

I once had a routine meeting with a donor just to catch up; there was no solicitation. During lunch, we chatted about the usual things—family, vacations and very little about the college, just in response to a question or two the donor had. I had no agenda and did not come close to asking for anything. When I took the donor home, she went to her office and came out with a check. I thanked her for the support but did not look at the check until I got back in my car. The amount had seven figures! When I returned to the office, I made an immediate thank you call (and then proceeded to tease the advancement staff that I was doing all of their work for them). It was one of those days that taught me an important lesson about donor relations.

8. Pay attention to heart and head

Making a charitable contribution of any size is an emotional decision. But donors also frame their decisions to give in a logical way that must make sense to them. My experience has been that, the larger the gift, the more heightened both emotions and logic become. There are times when we develop proposals for donors but do not adequately consider their perspective. We are so close to the situation and the needs of our institution that we forget to educate donors and understand their motivations for giving.

As with all relationships, the relationship between the donor and the college requires care and feeding. Once a gift is made, it is critical that the donor feels good about the experience and sees that the college is being a good steward of the gift by honoring the donor's intent. Your goal should not be to secure a one-time gift but to establish a lifelong partnership. That means you need to exceed the donor's expectation about the impact of the gift and the recognition he or she receives. The same is true if you are working with corporations or foundations. Empathy for the donor is a vital asset and should be shared among all faculty and staff.

Several years ago we were working with donors on a significant memorial gift in honor of a family member who had died at a young age. As with most significant gifts, it had taken some time to get everyone comfortable with the plan for the use of the funds. Once we had agreed in principle, we drafted a proposal that we thought reflected everyone's wishes. Our chief advancement officer met with the donors to review the draft of the plan. After the meeting, the advancement officer came back to campus in tears. The donors were very upset by some of the things we included; they did not understand why they were necessary and certainly did not believe they honored their family member properly. It was a challenging few weeks to overcome our mistake. The plan had made sense intellectually, but we failed to understand the donors' emotional state and to take into account their perspective. It all worked out in the end and was an instructive experience for us—especially for our chief advancement officer, who bore the brunt of the donors' immediate feedback. You and your team will make similar mistakes. What matters is how you respond to them and learn. If you are open and honest with your donors, they will trust you.

9. Remember why people give

Perhaps one of the biggest misconceptions about fundraising is what motivates people to give. The Lilly Family School of Philanthropy at Indiana University researched the topic and reported that the number one reason people give is ... because they are asked!

If you are not actively soliciting potential donors, you are missing a great opportunity. It also means that all of the people who are fond of your institution and the work you do are giving their money elsewhere—because you are not asking.

It's a simple concept, but I continue to hear from presidents that they find it difficult to ask for contributions. Many, I suspect, fear they will come across as weak or needy. Instead, take the opposite view; operate from a position of strength and success. First, there is no other organization like yours that has such a positive impact on individuals and communities. Your work provides lifelong benefits for people and is also a key driver of economic development. Although the work of other nonprofits is admirable, for the most part they only provide temporary or emergency intervention. Our work provides long-term solutions to some of our communities' most pressing issues. We have a great story to tell and can provide donors with incredible opportunities to make a difference with their contributions.

Sometimes we are reluctant to ask because we look at the contribution as a singular event. We think the donor's decision is whether to keep his or her money or to give it to us. The reality is that nearly all donors give a certain level of their assets to charitable causes. So the question in their minds is not whether to give, but which organizations to support. You are helping them to maximize the impact of their gifts. Potential donors are likely to give the funds somewhere, which is why asking is so important. Your work in advancement is about helping donors—who want to give—identify your college as an option for their philanthropy.

But you need to put the pieces in place ... and that means people. Advancement work is one of the few places where you can invest resources and see an almost immediate return on your investment. The more people you have, the more asks you can make. As time goes by, the return on that investment will grow exponentially. If you need proof, just look at TJC and the other community colleges that have invested in advancement work.

10. Believe!

The great industrialist Henry Ford once said, "Whether you think you can, or you think you can't—you're right." If you and your advancement team do not believe you can raise significant funds, you will not. I have used a lot of examples from TJC because that is the institution with which I am most familiar, having spent 25 years working there. We had extraordinary success raising funds. It really was and is the result of a wonderful advancement staff who believed in our institution and our ability to raise funds much like the more established four-year institutions.

I hear a lot of excuses from presidents and advancement officers about why they cannot raise funds like some other colleges. The excuses can include the wealth of the community, the size of the institution, the size of the advancement staff, lack of presidential involvement, a poor foundation board, and the like. TJC is typical by most measures. It is average in size, with approximately 8,000 students (headcount) during my time there. Tyler is an average-size city, with a population of approximately 80,000 and mostly rural counties surrounding the city that make up the college service area. There is not a lot of industry in the area. Despite being in the old East Texas oil field, wealth in our total service area is below average. So there are plenty of potential excuses for why we could not raise more money. But we didn't make excuses. We believed. We invested. And then we got to work.

Further, the top 100 community colleges in terms of funds raised per year and assets held in their support foundations is a widely diverse group on every variable. This means that success in advancement work is more about the people and less about circumstances. If you believe and if you commit yourself to advancement, your institution will be more successful ... and not just at raising money.

The public community college presidency is one of the most challenging jobs in education. Having been in that position, I know the demands on your time, your energy and your resources. Everyone wants more. A robust advancement operation requires more from you, but it also will provide resources and energy that will become contagious. Everyone, including you professionally, benefits. The only thing left to do is ask:

Shall we get started?

Section I

THE EARLY DAYS

Chapter 2

A COMMUNICATION STRATEGY FOR THE FIRST SIX MONTHS

By Carrie Besnette Hauser

For a newly appointed college president, nothing is more important than communication. Those within and around the institution are eager to hear your ideas, understand the direction you plan to take and observe how you will handle problems or take advantage of opportunities. Some will be natural skeptics. Others, immediate champions (and these roles may flip as time goes on). And, given the wide variety of constituent groups—faculty, staff, students, community leaders, legislators, board members, donors and other stakeholders—a new president must move between and among audiences carrying a consistent but appropriately tailored message.

This is the story of my first six months in office, having joined an institution that had been through a major leadership change and organizational upheaval prior to my arrival. The local media became a primary source of information and misinformation about the college for both internal and external audiences during a period of flux that had lasted nearly two years. Although a very capable interim president held the reins for part of this time, I arrived to find tensions high, trust compromised and relationships strained across the institution and within the communities we serve. My highest priorities were to calm the waters, ease concerns and build relationships. This meant being present, listening intentionally, and delivering and distributing information thoughtfully.

My institution is a complex entity. With a central administration office, 11 learning locations grouped into seven campuses, and a nine-county service area spanning 12,000 square miles (the size of Maryland) of the central Rocky Mountains, distance and sometimes-rugged terrain compound challenges to communicate effectively and consistently. I spent my first three months in a car, getting around to our various sites, taking time to know students, staff and faculty at each location; meeting with local community leaders and donors; and connecting with trustees and foundation board members—past and present. Some just wanted to be heard. Others were interested in my vision for the future of the institution.

Regardless of the circumstances a president finds when joining an institution, little is more important than choosing what to say and doing so consistently, knowing when or when not to relay a message, recognizing the occasions to listen and learn, modeling transparency in a variety of forms, and being genuine and authentic in every exchange, whether with internal or external constituents. Prioritizing audiences, the methods and frequency of communication and being willing to course-correct are also critical choices in the first six months.

What to communicate

Regardless of the institutional circumstances and environment a president inherits, a few tried-and-true messages should be relayed early on in a new presidency.

1. A reminder of history and the chapters that preceded you

Every institution has history and compelling stories to tell. Taking the time to understand the roots of a place, its evolution, key individuals or groups who helped it along and the cumulative impact it has had on students since its founding is important and worthwhile. Become the institution's newest and most knowledgeable historian. Take time to meet with former presidents, board members, donors, alumni and community leaders, and allow them to paint the picture and provide you with invaluable context. Then, relay key points to audiences you encounter. Many individuals in the college community, and certainly external constituents, may not know or recall why the institution was established in the first place, and if they do, there is no downside to a refresher and a little nostalgia.

Send a clear message that you are interested in the shoulders on which you stand, that you are one step in a long journey and that you have taken the time to understand the core and character of your institution so that you can help chart its next chapter.

Case in point: Once offered my position, I asked a few internal parties what became of the so-called founding father of our institution. I had read about him during my research and interview process and wanted to know more. After a little digging, I found out that he is approaching 90, is vibrant and healthy, and still lives in the state. We found time to get together; it was special and worthwhile for both of us. He felt honored and acknowledged. I was fortunate to learn of his journey and the history of my new institution from one of its original champions.

During our first occasion together, this extraordinary man handed me an old file folder of newspaper clippings, the college's first commencement program, recruitment materials that resulted in the hiring of the first president, photos and other priceless mementos. We stay in touch. I even invited him to my first hearing in front of the state's joint budget committee. Who better to introduce to a group of legislators, many of whom had no real understanding or recollection of the college's roots? One person's initiative nearly 50 years prior had resulted in the education of over a half-million students—a powerful mission and an inspirational story to share with others.

2. Confidence, vision and a shared purpose

Little is more important in a new presidency than instilling confidence, a clear direction and vision for the future, and a shared purpose. When an organization goes through change, particularly among top leadership, most stakeholders within the institution will ask themselves, "What does this mean for me?" Donors and partners will wonder if their investments and engagement will gain or lose traction. Board members are looking for their new leader to take charge and assess quickly the institution's challenges and opportunities.

Regardless of the circumstances that led the previous president to depart, there has likely been a period of transition, time for those who remain at the institution to reflect or wonder, and recognition that what was "known" under former leadership is no longer. For a new president, being visible is essential. Where and how you use your time is as key as any formal messages you might deliver, particularly early on.

Instead of spending the first day on the new job as many do—in the office, setting up a computer, filling out human resources paperwork, arranging your work space and getting oriented—consider another approach. If feasible, come in quietly the week or weekend before, when no one is around, to organize your office, test your technology, hang pictures, and do a "dry run" of your building, campus(es) and other surroundings.

Strategically and proactively plan in advance your first full day, week, and month of meetings and activities. By doing so, you can actually start working, versus "preparing to start," thereby sending a powerful message that you are ready to go with a sense of urgency about what lies ahead. Similarly, arrange to meet with students on day one. This will communicate with little question that they and their success are the top priority; all other efforts point to this "north star."

Case in point: At 9 o'clock on my first morning, the central office staff was invited to a coffee meet-and-greet. They welcomed me, and I welcomed them to the journey ahead. From that gathering, I went to meet with a group of students at one of our residential campuses. My only advance instructions had been that the group be a diverse representation of the student body and be willing to share with me a few things: their hopes and dreams, what they loved about their college and what they would change if they could. The session was meaningful, insightful and lasting. And, word got out. By the time I met with faculty members that same afternoon, my foremost commitment to students and their success was known. No first-day college-wide email or prepared speech could have been more effective and enduring. Several of the students I met with that first day helped form an official President's Student Advisory Council, which will serve as a sounding board for me during my tenure.

3. Consistency

Regardless of the message you are trying to communicate, above all else be consistent and never veer from the truth. In many ways, you are always communicating something somehow: verbally or nonverbally, by your behavior, how you dress, even your mood. Be self-aware and genuine in every interaction, or your credibility will fracture quickly. Internal and external audiences want assurance of your intentions and authenticity in all you do. In the early months of a presidency, you won't know everything about an institution, as you are in a listening and learning mode. But, how you present yourself and your "moral compass" will be scrutinized from your first appearance. Filters will be applied as humans hear what they want to hear. Consistency, clarity, repetition and reinforcement are the best antidotes to rumors and skepticism. As you build your knowledge base and begin to develop plans, stack new components onto initial messaging. Slowly and intentionally build momentum and invite others to join the cause.

Case in point: From my first day, my travel schedule, first impressions, key events and various interactions were shared with the entire college community. This level of sharing might seem unnecessary, but it set the tone and communicated that I would be open and honest with our various constituencies. It also helped establish trust and familiarity with my style when I needed to share more difficult news or changes within the organization. Confidentiality is appropriate or necessary at times, but a general tendency to share news, progress, challenges, direction—even mistakes—provides a solid foundation for effective relationships and healthy morale. This is particularly important if stunted communication or compromised information was the previous norm. It also reflects the organizational culture you seek to develop and models the behavior you expect from others.

When to communicate (and how often)

Although we communicate in some form or forms every day, the more formal messages are important to consider and calibrate in a new college presidency. Some leaders prepare a weekly update to share with employees. Others rely on direct reports and department heads to relay information across and through an organization. Whatever your style, be in tune to its effectiveness and regularity. And, whatever your approach, be prepared to maintain it or improve any standard, timetable or tone you set.

In my case, the idea of a weekly message did not resonate with my priorities. I planned to share information with some frequency, but to do so when it was most current and relevant, rather than on an artificially set schedule. For example, my communications included summaries of outcomes or actions taken after board meetings, an explanation of how a new fiscal year budget and increased health care costs would impact employee benefits and why, an invitation to provide input and be involved in a new strategic plan, and information on transitions within the organization as employees departed or joined. Minimally, a once-annual, "all-college," in-person gathering or town hall also serves as a norming exercise; everyone gets the same message, has the opportunity to ask questions and hears answers while together in the same location.

Above all else, model transparency. This concept can be overused and poorly implemented. Done well, however, transparency helps avoid a host of common problems, including the spreading of rumors and the breeding of suspicion. Simple and genuine gestures, like being in tune with people and their individual stories, and remembering names and faces, go a long way. In this regard, engaging every member of the governing board—and doing so equitably—is of utmost importance. What one board member knows, all should know. Triangulation, or going around one board member to another, will erode trust and relationships quickly.

Case in point: By their own description, the trustees of my institution were a divided group when I arrived. As many institutions experience, particularly when membership within the board changes, they had come to disagree about a number of issues. My immediate priority was to develop relationships with each individual trustee, to spend time with each in his or her home community, to call on them for advice, and to regularly communicate with the full group through electronic updates or otherwise. I routinely share with the board any all-college messages from me, so that they have a sense of my style and what is being communicated internally. This may appear to invite micromanagement, but the result has been the opposite. Board members quickly gained comfort in how information was being shared and could see that it was in sync with reports they received or their actions taken in board meetings. It also realigned the board with the institution's core work and mission—matters around which all could rally.

What not to communicate

Although a periodic and dependable flow of information from a new president is important and effective for reasons described earlier in this chapter, sometimes silence or delayed delivery is most appropriate. Facts and truth are essential. Wait another day or week if accuracy would otherwise be compromised. Saying "I don't know" or "I will share that information when I have it for you" is a perfectly suitable response.

Perhaps as obvious, but an area where carelessness can creep in, is articulating or passing critical judgment on past presidents, leaders of sister or neighboring institutions (or the institutions themselves), current or former trustees, employees or anyone else who may have had some association with the college. With varying motives or simply out of curiosity, some individuals may ask for your opinion on your predecessors, past employees, current ones who may be controversial, donors, board members or sensitive topics. Be careful. Weigh every response as if it will be repeated or translated in some form. The tried-and-true test is whether you would want something you say, do, or write to appear on the front page of the local newspaper. If not, don't say, do, or write it.

Case in point: The early months of my presidency coincided with the latest regulatory requirements of the Patient Protection and Affordable Care Act. Implementing the law without potentially causing negative impacts on part-time staff was a complicated undertaking. A local reporter was interested in the topic and how our college would be responding to the regulatory changes. He wrote an initial article that fell short of capturing the full picture and steps we were taking to address the matter. To ease anxiety among faculty and staff, I distributed an electronic communication to the entire college community outlining the issue, acknowledging its complexity, addressing how the college planned to phase in the new requirements and expressing my commitment to minimize any adverse impact on our faculty or staff. As part of an ongoing dialogue with the reporter, we alerted him to the memo and he requested a full copy, which we provided. Without our having criticized him or having asked him to correct his initial story, he wrote a follow-up article that was more thorough, balanced and—not surprisingly—included excerpts from the college-wide memo.

When to listen

Perhaps the most important communication tool in the first six months of a new presidency is to listen. There is as much to learn as there is to offer. In addition to asking as many thoughtful questions as you can, listening also means soliciting and receiving honest feedback. Develop relationships with a few valued individuals within the organization who will tell you the truth and keep you in tune with the pulse of the college and how your communication is received (or not).

The same is true for individuals and groups external to the organization. Tap a foundation board member, a key community leader or a former trustee to keep an ear to the ground and clue you in whenever a "touch" or appearance is needed. Keep a running SWOT (list of strengths, weaknesses, opportunities and threats) during your first 90 days, adding to it and noting themes that come up time and time again. Consider sharing it with key audiences to test or validate what you have heard.

Case in point: Several weeks prior to my start date, I issued a very brief "get to know you" survey to key individuals across my new institution, including direct reports, college leadership, trusted faculty members and select others—roughly 30 in total. Along with basic items like name, title, function, years at the college and hobbies, I also asked respondents to share their thoughts on these questions: What works best at the college? If you had a magic wand and money was no obstacle, what would you change? If you were starting your own company or new project, who are the three colleagues you would take with you and why? By organically learning about the institution and its people in the first few months and tallying the results of the survey, I developed a simple assessment of the SWOT that emerged.

Without attribution to any individual or source, I shared the results of my informal study at my 60-day mark with our college leadership council and invited them to react. It was a helpful and nonthreatening way to open discussion, to prioritize and to move forward with a common framework. And, because the SWOT was a report of what I'd heard from others, rather than my own words, it enabled employees to put their issues on the table anonymously and allowed me to verify (or modify) my own early assumptions, observations and research. I also shared the results with my governing board, again to model transparency and so that we were all on the same page from which to move forward.

With whom to communicate (and in what order)

The order and sequence of communication cannot be underestimated. With whom you meet and when can be at least as important as any message actually delivered. As noted earlier, I was intentional in meeting with students and faculty on my first day, as it established and clearly reflected my priorities. Several of these key individuals became ambassadors and credible internal allies as a result. I also made certain to research, understand and connect with the major political players, including donors and other key stakeholders, who were deeply invested in the college. Even those with whom I could not meet during my first 30 days because of scheduling conflicts knew of my intention to do so and that my scheduler was working on a time.

Case in point: There are plenty of folks who want to bend your ear, and their intentions may vary. Trust your gut. A few individuals internal to the organization reached out to me early on wanting a private meeting. Agendas are fine, but when they are presented behind closed doors or triangulated around other key players, they can be destructive, contaminate fact-finding or compromise transparency. In my case, I wanted to be approachable and to meet with a broad range of college and external constituents. If someone seemed to have a beef or was attempting to orchestrate an end-run, I first asked whether they had addressed the topic directly with the other parties involved. In several cases, I simply invited the other relevant players to join the meeting. Group knowledge or history seemed to mitigate one-dimensional perspectives and allowed many to weigh in on a given topic.

How (via what medium) to communicate

It is hard to recall the day not so long ago when hard-copy memoranda, campus mail, and the U.S. Postal Service were the standard options for communicating with an audience, small or large. Fast-forward to today. Now, brief messages or those that need instant, broad distribution are aided by modern technology. While enormously helpful in many instances, today's methods must be used with caution and discretion. Messages that you hope will have the recipients' full attention can get lost in overflowing inboxes. Errors or missteps, both major and minor, can quickly go "viral."

Whatever your style, select a few tried-and-true communication methods and use one or two only on rare occasions so that they stand out. Be consistent. If you send a weekly email (subject lines are critical), don't miss a cycle or some recipients may wonder why. And, as mentioned earlier, write and transmit everything with the awareness that it could end up on the evening news. I am not trying to provoke paranoia. Just be thoughtful, consistent and measured.

Lesson learned

For a new president, there is an eagerness to make a mark, set a tone, get everyone on the same page and move forward without delay. My greatest advice is to regulate this sense of urgency to some degree. Many constituents will be eager and wanting to adapt to your style, but you also need to meld into the institution. Give people time to adjust, change behaviors and adapt to a new direction. Like a molecule, made up of atoms, your institution is only as strong as the bonds that hold it together. Sometimes, the bonds take time and need to grow organically.

If I were to go back and modify one thing in my first six months, it would be to exercise more patience in certain areas. This is particularly true relative to my governing board. I am fortunate to work with a talented and committed group of individuals—elected officials who put themselves on a ballot to serve their communities and a noble cause. As a body, they had been through a challenging period and, by their own admission and accounts, had become fractured. Expecting them to unify in a few short months was unrealistic. And, any attempt on my part to influence their group dynamic was going to be premature, ineffective and frankly not a role a new president should take on.

So, together, we refocused on the basics—vision, mission, core values, guiding principles and, above all else, student success. My efforts and communication are similarly focused on these important fundamentals and on constantly reinforcing the institution's purpose and impact to all audiences—both internal and external.

What would I do again? Focusing on internal communication, being visible at our various campus locations, personalizing interactions and working from "inside out" proved very effective, given the needs of my college when I arrived. There were plenty of key occasions to meet with donors, volunteers, legislators, corporate partners and others in my first six months, but those inside and closest to the organization were my priority. This approach helped me to reestablish trust, seed a culture of openness and respect, and triage a long list of pending challenges and opportunities.

Developing a firm understanding of the organization and its infrastructure also aided my subsequent (and sometimes parallel) external messaging and relationship-building. Some new presidents conduct a media tour right out of the chute, but I used my first six months to prepare, build momentum and develop clear messaging for the press briefings and campus town halls that followed. Doing so helped me to more effectively tell the story of the institution, to describe the hurdles facing it and how we planned to respond, to ask for help from existing and potential partners, to advance a strategic plan and vision, and to become the college's chief spokesperson and champion.

Summary

Taking on a college presidency is simultaneously challenging, scary, energizing, exhausting and exciting. In few other arenas can one person meld organizational mission with personal passion and make such an impact. It is also a role played out in a fishbowl. What is said (both verbally and nonverbally)—and when, how and to whom—will never be more important or more scrutinized. And, in the first six months, the art of listening is perhaps the most effective tool in a new leader's toolbox.

Through effective and thoughtful communication, visions are formed, momentum is created, allies are forged and confidence is instilled. A careful assessment of the new environment, players and conditions is critical for calibrating the right messages and timing. Occasional mistakes will happen, along with abundant achievements. Remember to share and celebrate successes and recognize those who help move the institution forward. The president's job can be lonely at times, but there are countless others who will value your direction and communication style, join your team as a result and take your institution to new heights, all in the service of students. Above all else, consistency, authenticity, humility and honesty will carry the day.

Chapter 3

NEW HAT, NEW EXPECTATIONS

What New Presidents Need to Do
in Terms of Advancement in Their First Year,
and What They Should Expect From the Advancement Office

By DeRionne P. Pollard and David M. Sears

As a new community college president, you will wear hats you may never have worn before, such as chief fundraiser for your college. As you step into this particular role, there are critical steps you should take and expect your advancement office and college foundation to take with you.

It is all about setting and managing expectations, but it's not just about you. The chief advancement officer also plays an essential role in preparing you and the college for a successful transition. While there are specific, tactical things each person needs to do, success ultimately will depend on the quality of the relationship between the two, for one cannot be truly successful in fundraising without the other.

What to expect from the advancement office

Developing relationships with community leaders and stakeholders is a critical component of a new president's first-year success. Given the new president's myriad other responsibilities, the advancement office should take the lead and prioritize visits to those stakeholders as part of the presidential transition plan.

At Montgomery College, the transition plan covered three critical aspects: stakeholder visits, events to attend and presidential communications. The plan spanned six months, with visits delineated to be made in the first 30, 60, 90, 120 and 180 days of the new president's taking office. The advancement office was limited to three to five visits per month, taking into account that the president also needed to visit elected officials, community stakeholders and school leaders.

In the first 30–60 days, the president should expect that the advancement office is exposing him or her to top donors who will make the new president feel welcomed to the community. This is especially critical with new presidents with little or no fundraising experience. The advancement office is expected to ease the new president into the chief fundraiser role. Positive cultivation and stewardship visits from the start can help a new president embrace this role and actually enjoy it.

The president's perspective

DeRionne Pollard: At Montgomery College, the advancement office took me on several cultivation and stewardship visits to donors in my first six months. After a number of these visits, I made my first solicitation visit—a $750,000 ask of a donor whose family foundation had given over $2 million to the Montgomery College Foundation over the years. The advancement office made the visit seamless for me. First, they had a premeeting briefing with me to go over each person's role in the visit. As president, I would give the overview of the college, talk about recent activities and challenges and speak to the importance of giving. The program director followed my lead with a discussion of the business honors program and how successful the students had been in national business competitions and in running their own café. He also spoke to their high graduation rates and ability to transfer to four-year schools like Cornell, Columbia, New York University and Georgetown. The chief advancement officer handled the discussion of the gift opportunities, and I was able to make the specific ask with his coaching.

Second, they took care of all the logistics. For the visit, they set up the lunch at a place convenient to the donor but also at a restaurant I knew from previous visits to the area. They handled all the driving and directions, which eliminated that as a stressor prior to the visit—not an easy feat in Washington, D.C., area traffic.

Third, they had already done a lot of the legwork and prepped the donor for meeting me by providing my bio and information to him prior to the visit. The donor had Chicago ties, which helped the conversation flow naturally and put me at ease with the solicitation process.

The result of the preparation: a $750,000 gift from a family that was transitioning philanthropy from its patriarch to the family's next generation. It was the largest gift I had ever solicited and solidified my passion and enthusiasm for the chief fundraiser role. More important, going through the process and having the successful outcome gave me tremendous confidence that I would be able to solicit donors for transformational gifts.

Advancement expectations of the president

An advancement office's expectations for a president's involvement in their work remain relatively simple:

- The president will embrace the role of chief fundraiser;
- The president will be open to being trained on how to become a fundraiser;
- The president will make time for visits (3–5 per month);
- The president will communicate with donors and potential donors via various media and platforms; and
- The president will read the donor visit briefings and be prepared to follow the agreed-upon strategy and talking points for the visits.

The chief advancement officer's perspective

David Sears: From 2005 to 2009, I worked with two presidents with fundraising experience, Charlene Nunley and Hercules Pinkney, to raise $25 million for Montgomery College, the largest community college campaign in Maryland's history at the time. In 2010, with the arrival of DeRionne Pollard, I was concerned that she might be a fundraising novice, having come from a school that raised significantly less than Montgomery College's $3 million to $4 million per year.

Those fears were allayed quickly, as Pollard has consistently embraced and exceeded the five expectations of the advancement office. On every visit she has made with our director of development, Carol Rognrud, or me, she has read the briefings, followed our advice on the strategy and ensured that all of our talking points are covered before the meeting or visit is over.

At the beginning of the year, she provides the development office with set dates of her availability for donor visits and seldom changes her commitment to fundraise on those dates. Most important, Pollard's enthusiasm for advancement work is invigorating, and her passion shows in every conversation she has with donors and prospective donors. This passion also helps to boost the morale of the development staff to seek more gifts to support our students and programs, as they look forward to opportunities to make visits with the president.

Integrating plans with strategies

New presidents also should expect the advancement office to focus on asks and visits to prospective donors that tie into the college's strategic plan—and vice versa. Creating gift opportunities outside of the strategic plan can confuse donors as to what is most important to help the college reach its goals. It also makes it harder to implement the strategic plan and creates a scattershot approach to fundraising. Focus is critical.

As a new president, it can be enticing to want to just say yes to your first million-dollar gift and have that accomplishment to share with key stakeholders early in your tenure.

In the end, your trustees, key stakeholders and, ultimately, students will be better served by your wise decision to turn down a seven-figure gift outside of the strategic plan needs and focus on those gifts that will support the needs deemed most critical to student completion and success.

Our perspective

Pollard and Sears: At Montgomery College, we have turned down a donor twice who had offered a gift of seven figures because the intent of the philanthropy did not align with the strategic plan. It was not an easy decision, but it was the right decision. We had good conversations about why we should not accept the gift, how to speak with the donor about it, and what it meant for the fundraising efforts of the college's foundation and development office. We envisioned that a gift not aligned with the strategic plan would detract from efforts to fund initiatives within the strategic plan.

In the end, by declining the gifts, we were able to use the president's time and the college's resources more wisely by focusing on donors with interests that aligned with the strategic plan. The college's foundation and development office were still able to exceed their $3 million goal without the $1 million gift. The advancement office still cultivates and stewards the donor but continues to remind the individual and others that we are seeking gifts aligned to our five strategic plan themes.

Expectations for event attendance

Transition plans, briefings, communications, events and metrics are all intertwined as key tools for a new president to succeed in fundraising at a community college.

As noted earlier, the transition plan serves as the road map for the president, establishing key stakeholder relationships in a strategic and prioritized way. The transition plan also helps the president's gatekeeper to schedule and prioritize meeting requests, since so many stakeholders, both internal and external, want to meet the new president early in his or her tenure. By integrating event attendance into the transition plan, advancement officers can determine key stakeholders expected to attend a function and use the event as another way of ensuring the president meets key donors and leaders at events, as well as in one-on-one visits.

The president's perspective

Pollard: Montgomery College is a very president-centric institution, with so many internal and external stakeholders seeking a meeting with me in my first year. It was helpful to have the advancement office provide lists of which stakeholders might be attending a Chamber of Commerce dinner or a county event so that I could make well-informed decisions of whether I would meet one-on-one with certain individuals or accomplish the same goals with conversations at these events.

For each event, I would receive a briefing with mini-bios on those to be seated with me, as well as brief talking points with these individuals. Advancement officers did a great job in my first year, introducing me to people at events and bringing people to meet me so that we accomplished the goals for meeting stakeholders at the events. In the end, it was an excellent use of my time and a way to maximize the number of stakeholders I met in the first six months of my tenure.

Expectations for communications

Early, personalized communications also help set the stage for a new president's success as a chief fundraiser. A new president should expect that the advancement office is providing a communications plan that outlines which constituencies need early, consistent communications and via different media such as notes, emails, calls, tweets, etc. The office also ensures that the communications reflect the president's voice, style and tone and, most important, the key messages the president wants stakeholders to hear and embrace in his or her early tenure.

The advancement office expects that the president will be engaged with the communications process and be consistent in the messaging approach in speeches, letters, memos, etc. This is important not just for the internal constituencies, but also for external audiences to understand the messaging in their philanthropic, volunteer and advocacy efforts.

The president's perspective

Pollard: The advancement office and I were on the same page early regarding the need for communications to specific stakeholders. As a new president, I crafted handwritten notes to a select group of stakeholders whom I could not meet in the first 60 days as a way of connecting with them personally before an actual visit could take place. We developed improved communications processes with trustees and internal stakeholders to better engage them in the progress of the college and so that they could be better advocates and ambassadors in the community.

Metrics and expectations

A new president should expect the advancement office to be very metric centered. The chief advancement officer should always know about donors and dollars raised, but also about the number of visits expected to be made each month and to whom. The advancement office should also provide the president with monthly reports on the numbers and amounts of major gift proposals closed and outstanding. In this way, the new president has a way of measuring the effectiveness of the advancement office and keeping the staff focused on the business of philanthropy.

The chief advancement officer's perspective

Sears: Using fundraising metrics with a new president helps to show the science of fundraising and how the fundraising work is organized and run under best business practices. At Montgomery College, we have monthly donor and dollar reports to share with the president. We also consistently share the top major gift prospect list of who the president may be visiting, along with the analytics of the giving potential and capacity of the potential donor. This helps to frame the visit with the president and why the gift ask will only be in a certain dollar range. The more a new president can see the process at work and how metrics are used in deciding whom to visit and for how much to ask, the easier it is to explain the fundraising process.

Who does what during a visit

During a visit, a new president should expect the advancement officer to play two critical roles. The first is to serve as the recorder of the conversation. If the president makes a commitment to send the donor a book or an article, the advancement officer makes a mental note and handles that for the president as part of the follow-up strategy.

The advancement officer also ensures that conversations stay on track. Many advancement officers may wait far too long into a meeting or lunch to have the president make the solicitation. It is the advancement officer's job to keep the president on script throughout the visit. Although one of the goals of the visit is always to build the relationship, other goals are just as important, particularly if an ask is to be made for a critical academic program or scholarship initiative.

The president's perspective

Pollard: Success with visits can come in many forms. Recently, I made my first seven-figure ask of close friends of the college who had served on its foundation board and were highly respected in the community. The visit went flawlessly because I had been prepped well by the advancement officer on the specific ask amount, and I had read the briefing to know that the friends had recently been hospitalized and that certain conversations were to be avoided.

The preparation led to a delightful, focused conversation and a natural transition to the ask. The advancement officer played a critical role in "recording" the conversation, keeping us from drifting off topic, and being able to reiterate the next steps and ensure that my follow-up correspondence accurately reflected the conversation.

The result: a $1 million gift and, more important, a continuing relationship with these friends of the college.

Setting up success for year two and beyond

Obviously, it takes a lot of effort, preparation and time to engage a new president in his or her role as chief fundraiser for a community college. To continue momentum in the second and subsequent years, the president and development leadership should discuss the year's efforts and determine what is working well and what needs to be changed. This includes ensuring consistency of messaging with the stakeholders into the president's second year, and a continuous tie to strategic plan efforts. Review what is working well during visits and where they might improve. For example, a president or an advancement officer may point out how one or the other can better read the nonverbal cues of a donor or prospect. The conversation should also revolve around whom to meet in year two and a prioritization of the visits over the course of the year.

Our perspective

Pollard and Sears: One of the best things we can say about this process is that making visits together, in addition to solidifying our working relationship, actually helped us get to know each other much better. During the drive time to visits, you get the opportunity to pick the brain of the president, which not everyone at the institution gets to do on a regular basis. In this regard, it ends up being a special privilege to make the visits. You also get the chance to know each other as a person and not just by the person's title as president or senior vice president. It makes doing the work of fundraising that much more personal and rewarding. It also gives us the chance to laugh about things such as crazy events of the day; the bad driving habits of Washington, D.C., drivers compared to those of Chicago and Boston (our respective hometowns); and about all the engaging personalities of the community.

The time together and ability to share open and honest conversation is vital for us to be successful in our respective roles, and we now thrive on not just meeting but exceeding our mutual expectations.

Chapter 4

FINDING YOUR UNIQUE VISION AND PURPOSE

By Charlene Mickens Dukes and Brenda S. Mitchell

From its inception in 1958 as the first integrated school in the county, Prince George's Community College has been an agent of change. When I became the college's first female president in 2007, I was fortunate to have served as vice president under two popular and successful presidents. My move from vice president to president was not uncommon in community college circles. More than a third of community college presidents ascended to their office at institutions where they were already serving, although most come from academic positions rather than student services, as I did.

While I, of course, wanted to do some things differently, I realized that I was not hired to be a change agent. With an already-committed focus on student success, as evidenced in the college's strategic plan, I faced a different challenge: How would I effectively transition from within the college as its new leader, build on the good work of my predecessors and shape a unique vision for the future of the institution?

There were inherent advantages to this arrangement. I had a level of familiarity and comfort with the institution—our vision, mission and strategic direction. I knew the faculty, staff, administration and the board of trustees—and they knew me. As a county resident, I was already active in local organizations and acquainted with community and business leaders. Because of this, my orientation consisted not so much of learning about the institution and the community we serve, but of defining my new role within it.

Yes, I had on my side the momentum gained by my predecessors, but I knew that the status quo could not support the college's rising prominence. Having worked with both presidents as a member of their cabinets, I understood the existing challenges as well as the opportunities. Whether making wholesale or incremental changes, I needed to consider and identify the institution's unique niche and vision and be able to articulate it clearly.

Prince George's Community College began in 1958 with 185 students and 14 part-time faculty members. The college relocated to its main campus on 150 acres in Largo, Maryland, in 1967. More than half a century later, the student population has grown to over 44,000, representing more than 100 nationalities. In 2011, *Community College Week* named Prince George's Community College one of the 50 fastest-growing public two-year colleges in the nation. With an additional six extension centers, the college's offerings are now available to citizens throughout the county.

I arrived at Prince George's Community College in 1995 as vice president for student services. In that position, I worked with two presidents, Robert I. Bickford, who served the institution for a total of 37 years, and his successor, Ronald A. Williams, who became president in 1999.

A history of growth and success

Bickford, who led Prince George's Community College for 27 years, was a steady, constant presence during a period of high growth and expansion. During his presidency, enrollment more than tripled, the number of academic programs doubled and the budget increased more than sixfold. While most four-year institutions had a long and well-established tradition of philanthropic giving, community colleges typically did not.

Because community colleges were conceived as publicly supported institutions, little thought was given initially to their need for additional private funding. However, the seeds of change for our college were planted during Bickford's presidency with the creation of the Prince George's Community College Foundation in 1985. Perhaps because they still believed private gifts would be difficult to garner, the foundation originally focused its efforts internally, with a board made up largely of faculty and staff. Regardless, the foundation was up and running, and faculty and staff involvement and buy-in continues to pay dividends today.

When he assumed the presidency in 1999, Williams made it a priority to raise the public profile of the college, emphasizing academic excellence, quality and achievement of national prominence. Perceiving the college as the intellectual hub of the community and vital to the well-being of the county, Williams spoke often of the college as an economic engine for workforce development. All of his initiatives produced results. The college received a number of accolades from national organizations, including the Association of American Colleges and Universities, which named Prince George's Community College as one of 16 institutions serving as models of best practice in liberal education. The college's work became more visible through partnerships with outside groups, increased public outreach, and a concerted marketing and public relations campaign. Three new extension centers helped to expand the college's geographic reach.

From the outset, Williams faced resource challenges. Concerned about the instability of public funding, he pushed to accelerate fundraising from private sources. The foundation, despite having been in operation for more than a decade, was still in its infancy. Williams oversaw a transformation of the board, recruiting external members, many of whom were well known locally. In this way, he was able to both promote public awareness of the college and raise support for its work.

Under Williams's leadership, the college launched its first major gifts campaign in 2004. Centered on the theme "Changing Lives ... Building Communities," it was the institution's largest fundraising effort to date. Williams received a warm reception throughout the community, which he justifiably attributed to the positive impact of our programs and services on the lives and livelihoods of county residents and businesses. Before its conclusion in 2007, the campaign had exceeded its goal of $6 million and the college's endowment had more than doubled. Two major facilities, the Center for Advanced Technology and the Center for Health Studies, were in the early stages of construction and design.

When Williams announced his resignation in 2006, it came as a surprise to many. While he reviewed the achievements of his presidency, he acknowledged that a very real obstacle remained: inadequate funding. During his tenure, the college had raised tuition—a difficult decision given the institution's commitment to affordability. As Williams departed, there was a sense that the college could truly prosper with access to the full range of resources it deserved and required. We had tested the waters with the major gifts campaign but were still far from sophisticated in our development strategy. Even so, we were off to a great start.

In the beginning: Unexpected hurdles

After a national search, I assumed the role of president in July 2007. Early in my presidency, a confluence of events forced me to hit the ground running. The first year, 2007–2008, marked the beginning of a devastating financial crisis that would affect economies and governments worldwide. It impacted us directly and immediately. Budgets that had been tight became tighter. At the same time, enrollment spiked. In the fall of 2009, we had our largest credit enrollment in 25 years as the college became more attractive to those looking for an affordable education, hoping to upgrade their skills or retrain for new careers. While the influx of students would mean at least a temporary increase in tuition revenue, it also highlights issues such as capacity, staffing, scheduling, support services and curriculum development.

My challenge was to create a vision and direction for the college that respected my predecessors but also enabled me to address key issues. I identified three areas of emphasis, each of which also had ramifications for the entire college: branding and communications, student success and resource development. The most important thing a president can do is shine a spotlight on a college priority, but that also requires focus, determination and a willingness to say no to other things.

One of my first major undertakings as president was to create a branding strategy that would be used to connect and communicate with our students and other stakeholders in a clear and concise manner, as well as to build on our credibility within the community. Our branding campaign, "Transforming Lives," was successful in positioning Prince George's Community College as a leader in higher educational opportunities in the county and region. The new brand was also used to highlight specific academic, workforce development and continuing education programs to various audiences primarily through advertisements in seven major venues: newspaper/magazine, radio, television/cable, mass transit, outdoor, Internet and movie theaters. That message continues to be communicated through the college's major publications such as the annual report, schedules of classes, catalog, viewbooks and student success posters on the campus.

Coming from a student services background, I viewed student success as our top priority and one of the toughest to tackle. Our highest-achieving students were thriving in programs such as the Honors Academy, which offered financial support and academic enrichment. But as an open-access institution, we serve many students for whom persistence is difficult. The college has long faced a lack of academic preparedness on the part of incoming students, an issue that puts a strain on institutional resources and an even greater burden on the students. More than three-quarters of students entering Prince George's Community College qualify for one or more developmental courses. This need for remediation greatly impedes student progress.

With a successful brand in motion, I felt the college was ready to address the issue of student completion through a formal institution-wide plan we called "Envision Success." Research has shown that completion is enhanced through optimization of time spent on campus, directed choices and more structured scheduling. By systematically gathering and using data, Envision Success is improving or developing support services, academic programs, and workforce development and training programs to assist students at every stage of their educational journey. This involves continual assessment, accountability and action as we work to create the conditions most likely to promote student success.

I also wanted to strengthen the institution organizationally, by investing in people and infrastructure, opening clear lines of communication, and governing in a transparent and inclusive manner. With Envision Success and all aspects of institutional planning, our decision making is supported by extensive research. Shortly after I became president, we integrated our assessment, budgeting and planning procedures and linked them to our strategic initiatives in order to remain on track with our priorities and allocate resources efficiently and appropriately. This gives us measurable outcomes and provides accountability.

Building momentum through philanthropy

As a vice president, my participation in development activities had been limited, but as president, I became the college's chief fundraising officer. I knew that to ensure as seamless a transition as possible, I would need to reach out to the foundation board quickly. I wanted to ascertain where we stood and how we could proceed together in the best interests of the college. Within weeks of taking office, I met individually with each serving board member. I shared with them my background and my thoughts on the direction of the college. Though I had grown professionally under the leaderships of Bickford and Williams, I hoped to step out and craft a new and expanded vision for the college, building on the work they had begun. In my view, the foundation would play an integral role in that vision. I offered each member the opportunity to remain with the organization. In the end, 100 percent of the board members chose to stay on.

As I took office, Prince George's Community College was poised to celebrate its 50th anniversary. It was a time of reflection and celebration, but also a moment to consider where we were headed and how to get there. The progress made over the previous eight years had given us significant momentum; now we had to capitalize on it. Our first major gifts campaign was successful in raising public awareness of the college's work and its value to the community. The endeavor led to a number of new alliances with businesses and initiated important relationships with prospective donors in the county. It broadened the scope of our fundraising efforts, moving us from simply an annual giving model to more of an emphasis on long-term strategic collaborations.

We saw that there was interest from the community. We had an engaged board. The campaign demonstrated the potential for a much more proactive and robust approach to development. Under the leadership of its executive director, Brenda S. Mitchell, the Office of Institutional Advancement underwent a major reorganization to support the new demands of the office. The office is now better equipped to provide leadership, consultation and other support on strategic externally funded or sponsored projects that support the vision, mission and strategic priorities of the college. The staff works hard to position the college to be an outstanding intellectual resource for education welfare and economic development that is of high value to the college's stakeholders. But to maximize the utility and effectiveness of foundation activities, it was first necessary to align them with the activities of the college. This was a new idea for both the foundation and the college.

The college's priorities are articulated in its strategic plan and augmented by assessment and budgeting procedures. The foundation, however, had never been through an independent strategic planning process and thus lacked a formal mechanism for setting goals and determining progress. In 2009 the board completed its first strategic plan, which allowed for a streamlined and synchronized approach to planning and methodically delineated the board's role in supporting the college.

Among the plan's strategic goals was to enhance the foundation's function as the advancement arm of the college. Board members felt that they lacked a consistent and clear charge and an understanding of the long-term vision for the foundation. They saw a need for better communication, greater synergy with staff, increased resources within the foundation and improved public perception of the institution. These concerns were valid and indicative of an organization that was just beginning to find its way. In articulating areas of perceived weakness, the foundation board was outlining concrete ways in which we could better equip them to help us. The strategic planning process was valuable in setting clear priorities and objectives, but it also spoke to the board's enthusiasm. They had defined their role and were ready to get to work.

We recognized that our foundation board members were an untapped resource and set about empowering them. The easiest way to improve public perception of the college is to make people aware of all that we do. In this regard, our foundation board members are terrific ambassadors. They have taken their roles as philanthropic leaders to heart. The president is the public face of the college, but I cannot be everywhere all the time. We need help getting the word out, and it's often more effective when it comes via a peer-to-peer encounter. Board members, most of whom are leaders in the local business community, have personal and professional relationships throughout the region. Through these contacts, they are able to take our story further than we ever could on our own.

Consequently, the foundation has expanded beyond its board and staff. It now consists of an enthusiastic network of volunteers who meet regularly to offer guidance, plan events and recruit others. We now have several spinoffs or subgroups dedicated to various aspects of development. These individuals are all volunteers who came to us through contacts we gained in the business community. We have experienced many "aha" moments in which people who had only a vague familiarity with the college changed their perceptions dramatically. When they learn about the scope of our programs and services, they see the possibilities for collaboration and want to offer their support and time.

Foundation board members have a vested interest in the success of the college. Many live in Prince George's County; others have businesses located here. Nearly all have employees who live in the county. They see firsthand the benefits the college offers the community by providing comprehensive, affordable education and relevant training. Their unique strengths and wealth of professional expertise are a tremendous asset to the institution. Rather than simply lending their names to the foundation, our board members are actively engaged in hands-on work, taking meetings, making calls, participating in events, networking and strategizing. They are able to relay our message so effectively because they believe in it. Every board member also is a donor.

Our volunteers' time and input are valuable, and we try to respond accordingly. These are busy people, and we want to make the most of their participation. Seemingly small touches, like meetings that start and end on time, are important. If someone brings a suggestion to the table or mentions a name, we will follow up in a timely manner. When our volunteer leaders are out in the community, we make certain they are well prepared to represent the college. We want to make the experience worthwhile for them and offer some value-added incentive. They appreciate our attention to what might be called "the efficiency factor."

Embarking on a second campaign

With a rejuvenated board in place, we were able to launch a second major gifts campaign in 2011. "Purpose, People, Possibilities" raised funds for three institutional priorities: scholarships and student services, academic and workforce development programs, and facilities and modern equipment for teaching and learning. By identifying areas of need that corresponded to the college's institutional priorities, the campaign aimed to increase resources for current programs and services and encourage expansion and innovation. The campaign was the vehicle by which we would realize the objectives set forth in Envision Success.

The foundation board immediately took ownership of the enterprise. The leadership team set the strategy for the campaign, took the lead in making personal gifts, and fostered external momentum. The campaign's success was far beyond our expectations. Within its first year, it raised $18 million, surpassing the initial goal of $15 million. At the foundation's 2012 Partners for Success awards dinner, the president of the foundation and I announced a new campaign target of $25 million. When we exceeded this second, higher goal by raising more than $31.8 million, it was a testament to the tireless work and advocacy of our campaign leadership team, along with the support and dedication of the entire foundation board. In addition to taking the message to the public, they reached out to faculty and staff through the Office of Institutional Advancement, organizing meetings to introduce employees to the campaign and solicit internal buy-in for its goals. As a result, employee giving increased and many departments achieved 100 percent participation.

An empowered board led to increased autonomy. Previously, the college president was primarily responsible for recruiting new board members. Now the board is identifying and recruiting suitable candidates on its own. The foundation's second and recently completed strategic plan gives greater consideration to board development and recruitment, with the aim of increasing the diversity and size of the board. To acknowledge the foundation's identity as separate and distinct from the college, the plan seeks to publicize the work of the organization with both internal and external audiences. It is a proactive plan that reflects the foundation's expanded reach and ability to leverage resources in support of the college. This includes keeping abreast of changes taking place within the county and identifying sectors and businesses that could serve as future collaborators.

Keeping an eye on the horizon

Even as one campaign comes to an end, there is always another on the horizon. Our volunteer campaign leadership team, whose work was so successful, was not fixated solely on meeting a number goal. They realized that even when we reached our target, the college would continue to have funding needs. They are thinking strategically, with a view to the long-term financial stability of the college.

Our main Largo campus is more than 40 years old. Remodeling is a constant theme. Once buildings are renovated or built, they must also be furnished and outfitted with current equipment. The acquisition and upgrading of technology is a constant need. In addition to the projects we have planned, we must also anticipate the unexpected. Flexibility is an institutional strength, but to adapt to changing circumstances, we must have a strong and secure base.

While ours and other community college foundations began as small subsidiaries of their institutions, under the direction of college presidents, they have now moved away from that ancillary role. There is an understanding that these organizations should be self-sustaining and working alongside, rather than simply under, the college's leadership. It is a symbiotic relationship. Part of a president's job is to inspire and motivate. Volunteers want and need to know what they are working for and why. Donors need to feel their contributions are making a real difference. It is less about the ask and more about presenting the case, telling the story. People who hear our well-told story want to be part of it.

When the Prince George's Community College Foundation was created in the mid-1980s, it was with the notion that private funding could be beneficial and that people with close ties to the college, such as alumni and employees, might be willing to contribute. Even back then, foundation organizers knew that to be successful, the institution would need to shift its focus outward, to think bigger and be more ambitious.

In partnership with the foundation board, we took that thought and developed it more fully around our purpose—why we are here in the first place and what we do best. We now know that fundraising can no longer be confined to small-scale annual giving or even to the occasional major gifts campaign, although both will continue. Large-scale fundraising is now an integral part of the college's operations. Our volunteer leaders have achieved extraordinary success and, through careful cultivation and recruitment, will help ensure similarly qualified successors.

I believe that the work we are engaged in now will sustain the college well into the future. Prince George's Community College has always had as its mission the transformation of lives through education. To effect change, we must be able to undergo change. We must envision where we would like to go and mobilize a plan, to include others beyond our walls, and to execute in order to meet our community's and our students' evolving needs. Change requires momentum and resources. The momentum is with us, the vision is ours and with those things intact, the building of resources continues successfully.

Section II

BOARD DEVELOPMENT AND RELATIONSHIPS

Chapter 5

CONNECTING THE DOTS

Aligning District and Foundation Priorities

By Rufus Glasper

As in many state systems and districts, a hallmark of the Maricopa County Community College District has been our ability to rapidly respond and grow to meet our community's learning needs. Consistent with the early years of "junior colleges," our first campus—now known as Phoenix College—developed as a result of burgeoning numbers of area high school students who lacked convenient opportunities for postsecondary education. Today, our district consists of 10 individually accredited colleges, two skill centers, a corporate college, and multiple satellite extensions that educate and train more than 224,000 students who take credit courses and 32,000 who are enrolled in non-credit, special interest courses each year.

As the population grew over the years and individuals moved farther from the center of Phoenix proper, colleges were organized to serve a six-mile radius and were encouraged to organize in a quasi-independent manner. The central office provided support services, leaving the colleges to grow and expand in response to the needs of their constituents. That means our 10 community colleges each developed a broad spectrum of programs, facilities, and business and community partnerships. A diffuse organizational structure, encouraged during the early and middle years of the district, served us well, but its limitations now outweigh its benefits.

Unfortunately, that quasi-independent structure resulted in significant competition between our colleges for students, for funding and for programmatic partnerships such as clinical lab space for health care and nursing students. Decentralization also created challenges for fundraising and development, with multiple entities representing the district, our colleges and the foundation, knocking on the same doors and passing each other in the same halls of potential donors. Given the "bootstrap" mentality that enabled community colleges to grow, I see this as an issue not only in large districts, but also between departments at the smallest community colleges.

College autonomy within our system left gaps in (and on occasion resistance to) system-wide planning and coordination, which has led to some duplication of services and internally disruptive competition among colleges. These historical patterns, however, provide opportunities for change and improvement that our district needs to undertake in order to thrive in the years ahead. Our strategic plan addresses these gaps, and we already have much progress and success to report.

The chancellor's three pillars

In mapping out our future, I have relied on three pillars to guide our strategic thinking and organizational change. These three pillars are student success, stewardship and ONE Maricopa. For this book's readers, there is no need to expand on the pillar of student success, but suffice it to say that it is my expectation that everything we do, in some way, advances the success of Maricopa students. The pillar of stewardship serves as a constant reminder to all employees that, more than a job, their work is an exercise in trust placed on them by the students and taxpayers of Maricopa County. The third pillar, ONE Maricopa, is the guiding principle of the Maricopa Community Colleges—representing the notion that we have 10 outstanding colleges and now a corporate college, each serving its own community but working together when it makes the most sense to do so.

ONE Maricopa is driven by our changing environment and is embraced by internal and external stakeholders as a means to enhance student success, though at times it is hampered by historical contexts. It is not a mandate or a nonnegotiable but rather a cultural shift that is gaining understanding and acceptance, as well as an appreciation of the benefits to students and the community. This shift has not been easy for a district that has grown and developed based on principles of entrepreneurship and competition.

Tactically, implementation of ONE Maricopa includes the following:

- open, collaborative conversation and speedy decision making to the greatest extent possible;
- dynamic interactions between and among the district office and the colleges, with everyone operating from shared guiding principles;
- greater standardization across all of Maricopa when it makes sense;
- strategies that promote student success across the system;
- decision making that balances effectiveness and efficiency with individual college identity; and
- a culture that supports innovative teaching and learning.

Because the Maricopa Community Colleges evolved based on a geographical model, many of our operations have been decentralized. Historically this decentralization has been valued, since it fostered innovation. However, decentralization has inhibited system-wide innovation, specifically in the areas of fundraising and development.

Maricopa and the fourth revenue stream

Consistent with other private and public entities, the Maricopa County Community College District has had to adapt to the impact of the Great Recession and the slow recovery. For a number of years prior to 2008, we had focused on adding a fourth revenue stream, adding to our long-standing "three legged stool" of property taxes, state aid, and tuition and fees. However, since 2008–2009, we have had to absorb a 99 percent decrease in state aid, which had historically made up the third leg of the stool. In developing the fourth revenue stream, we were (and still are) actively engaged in diversifying our revenue sources. One of the changes I made was to increase our college presidents' responsibility for fundraising and development.

Until the early 2000s, the presidents of our 10 colleges did not have a formal responsibility for fundraising. They had not been hired with that expectation, most of them did not have fundraising experience and it had never been a priority. Some were excited by the idea; others were not, since the Maricopa culture pushed presidents to be focused internally. Spending time off campus for any reason was not viewed positively by many on our campuses. There is truth in the cliché that "what gets measured gets done," so in 2008 I made fundraising one of the items in the presidents' evaluations. This was designed

- to let the presidents and the wider college and district communities know that I was serious about fundraising as a priority and that they needed to be as well;
- to motivate the presidents to become better prepared and more active as fundraisers; and
- to provide the presidents with some "cover" on their individual campuses as they moved to spend more time off campus and in the community.

Maricopa is advancing rapidly in a number of areas. We continue to expand job training options, which included the creation of a corporate college to provide credit and noncredit economic workforce development offerings. We are expanding online learning partnerships with other colleges and universities, as well as high schools within and outside the state. And the Maricopa Community Colleges Foundation has launched a new, comprehensive fundraising campaign.

The Maricopa Community Colleges Foundation: Background and history

The Maricopa Community Colleges Foundation was created in 1977 by a group of Maricopa Community College employees. The founding employees served as the foundation's first board, and its first executive director was appointed in the summer of 1980. The organization's assets at the time totaled $4,466, only $1,100 of which was in cash.

The foundation grew rapidly, with a series of campaigns with increasingly ambitious goals. An initial fundraising effort in 1982 resulted in $220,000 in unrestricted funds. Just six years later a second campaign concluded with pledges to build an endowment of $3 million. A second phase of that campaign raised another $3.2 million, for a total of over $6.2 million. This allowed the foundation to distribute some 6,500 scholarships over the next five years.

From 1996 to 1999 another campaign was undertaken, raising another $12.8 million, providing for thousands of new scholarships. In 2002 the foundation decided on a campaign to expand and support the district's very successful Achieving a College Education (ACE) program. That campaign concluded in 2008, having raised $8 million to expand the ACE program to all 10 of the Maricopa Community Colleges. By the time the ACE campaign ended, the foundation had a staff of about a dozen, a board of directors that had been in place for some time and assets of around $25 million, of which 80 percent was in endowed funds.

Transition and change in the foundation

As the district and foundation were concluding the ACE campaign, it became clear that changes were needed in the foundation. The foundation board had been in place for many years, and while the board members were great supporters of and advocates for the district and the foundation, they had never really been asked to be fundraisers, nor did they see that as their role. Further, the foundation staff had become somewhat complacent, as several million dollars a year came in without much effort. This inhibited the ACE campaign and suggested that we were not ready for the future that was coming. We needed to change.

The foundation's CEO at the time and the vice chancellor for student and community affairs developed an initial plan in two parts. The first part—developed in cooperation with the board leadership—was a complete overhaul of the foundation board. The reasoning was simple: Start at the top and develop a board that would lead change. The second part was to prepare for the coming change by hiring a consultant (not the first) to assess the organization and help us through the transition. Wide-ranging discussions ensued about what we wanted the new board to look like and what we would expect of it. After considerable discussion, we agreed that we wanted a board that was

- diverse (along a number of dimensions),
- committed to active engagement,
- committed to fundraising, and
- committed to personal giving.

The foundation board now has between 24 and 30 externally elected directors, and eight *ex officio* directors, including the chancellor, two members of the elected district governing board and three college presidents.

The board meets five times a year. Because we assumed—correctly so—that an active and engaged board would have more to do, a committee structure was created to facilitate the board's ability to conduct business. Each committee is chaired by a member of the executive committee and meets as needed. The committees are

- Strategic Planning (chaired by the board chair),
- Fundraising (chaired by the board vice chair),
- Finance, Investments and Audit (chaired by the board treasurer),
- Scholarship (chaired by the board secretary), and
- Board Development (chaired by the immediate past board chair).

Each board member serves on at least one committee, is a part of some effort of the fundraising committee and is involved with the review of scholarship applications. The board also formalized a set of board member expectations that are shared with and agreed to by every board member and candidate for the board.

Service on committees was just one of the new expectations for board members. Other expectations include attendance at a new member orientation on being elected to the board, attendance at a minimum of three board meetings each year, a minimum annual gift (currently $1,200), a personal campaign gift, and active involvement in the process of friend- and fundraising.

While the changes in the foundation board were under way, we also elevated the status of the foundation within the district by naming the president and CEO of the foundation as a vice chancellor and a member of the Chancellor's Executive Council. The foundation almost immediately moved into new offices in a separate building both to give it more visibility and to enhance its identity as a quasi-independent organization. A memorandum of understanding defining the relationship between the district and the foundation was signed by the two boards, and a significant assessment and reorganization of the structure and staff began. The organization was restructured and that restructuring continues.

Aligning district and foundation priorities for the next campaign

As the board, the staff and the organization continued to transform, the notion of a new and significant campaign was explored. Following a feasibility study, the foundation board voted to undertake a four-year, $50 million campaign, by far the largest in the foundation's history—and among the largest ever by a community college or district. "The Campaign for Student Success" is a significant effort to align the district's larger priorities, specific college priorities and the foundation's fundraising mission.

As chancellor, I am an *ex officio* member of the foundation board and provide a district update at each meeting. These in-depth presentations always result in numerous questions and robust conversation. Thus, as decisions were being made about the campaign, the foundation was well aware of two of my most important priorities: a focus on student success and the principle of ONE Maricopa.

The Maricopa Community Colleges were not alone in viewing student success as a goal of singular importance. The foundation board determined that aligning both the foundation and the campaign with this goal was the appropriate thing to do. To do so, three areas of focus within the campaign were developed. The first was direct support for students to help them be successful. This included scholarships of all sorts, support for internships and support for other kinds of activities that directly benefit students. The second area of focus was support for faculty and staff efforts to improve student success. This included things like applied and classroom research, student research opportunities, and opportunities to send students to attend and present at conferences. The third area of focus was on community partnerships that could positively affect student success. Included were various partnerships with K–12 schools, employers and community organizations.

For many years and for many reasons, the 10 Maricopa Community Colleges operated independently and often competitively. We have always had one foundation, but tensions arose at times between the foundation and the colleges, which wanted to act independently. As a result, not all of the money raised at the colleges wound up in the foundation. The previous campaign had been developed with more of a top-down approach, with the colleges "invited" to participate. Some colleges with a large stake in the campaign had been enthusiastic participants; others with less interest, less so. We were well aware of this and determined that the new campaign would actively involve the colleges from the start and would be built on the ONE Maricopa principle.

Once a feasibility study was completed and the themes that would resonate with the community were clear, we began to involve the colleges in the creation of fundraising goals and the development of projects for each college that were consistent with those goals. First, a visioning session was held at each college, facilitated by foundation staff and campaign counsel. Each college president convened a group of internal and external stakeholders to participate in a structured exercise to select projects—consistent with the student success theme—for which the college wanted to raise money in the campaign. Following this activity the colleges were then charged with developing the details and the cost for each project.

The result of this effort was a document titled "Opportunities for Investment," which listed every campaign project by college and by one of the three areas of focus. This booklet, along with the campaign case statement, has been our primary resource in approaching donors. In addition, since all of the projects can be found in one place, every fundraiser—from the college presidents and development officers to foundation board members—is aware of every project. A donor may be approached about a specific project, perhaps for one college, but if the donor's interest is elsewhere, in a different project at a different college, perhaps, the fundraiser can shift focus to that project.

We have found that this encourages a ONE Maricopa approach and reinforces the notion that what is good for one is good for all. As the above example illustrates, fundraising responsibility in the campaign can be somewhat diffuse and occasionally confusing. However, we have tried to define that shared responsibility, consistent with the ONE Maricopa notion that some things are best done centrally, others regionally and still others at the local college level.

As chancellor, I am the district's principal fundraiser, and my prospects include, for the most part, the largest companies in the community and their CEOs. Their interests are typically community-wide: scholarships for students and support for programs at all the colleges. Occasionally, however, a corporate donor will have an interest in a specific program or project at a single college (or several colleges). Depending on the prospect, I may be supported by a foundation board member, a member of the foundation staff or a particular college president.

The foundation board also has community-wide fundraising responsibility in the campaign. Using their own individual and business contacts, foundation board members are cultivating prospects for district-wide projects as well as those at specific colleges, consistent with their prospects' interests. When appropriate, they are also involved in the solicitation of the companies for which they work. In their fundraising work, they are often supported by one of the foundation's development staff.

Each college president, with the support of that college's development officer, is responsible for raising money for the college's projects in the campaign. They receive support, as needed, from their colleagues at other colleges when a regional approach is called for, as well as from foundation board members and staff. My expectation is that approximately 30 percent of the presidents' time is spent on fundraising and development.

Relationships are at the core of our current fundraising efforts. No individual or any unit in the Maricopa Community Colleges is working independently on the campaign. We are making a concerted effort to run the campaign in a manner consistent with a ONE Maricopa perspective, and to use the campaign to help further that perspective.

Successes and challenges

Consistent with community colleges nationally, Maricopa Community Colleges are continuing to evolve. Specific to what the foundation does and its relationships with the district office, we can report some continued challenges and successful outcomes as well. First, the successes:

- For the most part, we have successfully "connected the dots." Student success is the district's number one priority, and the foundation has embraced this goal enthusiastically, focusing its current campaign on student success. Indeed, the campaign originally was called "Educating Our Community, Ensuring Our Future" but was rebranded as "The Campaign for Student Success," to make that commitment even more explicit. Every effort has been made to think of and conduct the campaign from a ONE Maricopa perspective.
- The transformation of the foundation board into a more formidable body has been an advantage both to the foundation and to me, and it helped set the stage

for greater alignment between the foundation and the district. Foundation board members are well respected in the community and that respect can be leveraged externally as well as internally.

- Much of the foundation's commitment to student success and ONE Maricopa comes from two important relationships. The first is my own relationship to and involvement with both the executive committee and the board itself. I am very much a part of the foundation board, and they feel very much a valued part of the district. Second, the fact that the foundation's president and CEO is also a vice chancellor has been important. Our campaign has expanded and enhanced my role as a fundraiser, and the community is coming to see me (and the office of the chancellor) as a fundraiser. That is a shift that should bode well for the future.
- My fundraising efforts require considerable support from the district and foundation leadership. The working relationship around that support has been strong and positive.
- Finally—and although more remains to be done—the culture in our district around fundraising and the role of leadership in fundraising is starting to change, which is essential to our future success.

Our successes also suggest some of our challenges, which include the following:

- Old habits, old ways of doing business and a culture built up over decades all die hard. Competitiveness and, in some cases, lack of cohesion between the colleges, between the colleges and the foundation, and even between the colleges and the district office were built up over those decades. Although we are moving steadily, if slowly, away from that culture, it continues to linger in different places and at different times.
- Similarly, ONE Maricopa is taking hold across the district, but it is a cultural shift that takes time. This is true for our campaign as well. Some of our colleges are fully engaged in the collaborative nature of the campaign; others are approaching fundraising more independently.
- As stated previously, I've made fundraising a goal for our presidents and one on which they would be evaluated. That is not like waving a magic wand. Presidents who came to their positions with no expectation that they would have to raise money and with no experience in doing so, at colleges with little or no fundraising success, do not become highly experienced and successful fundraisers overnight. This is an ongoing process made even more challenging by a historical culture in which presidents were focused much more internally than externally.
- Finally, regardless of the progress we may have made in becoming a better, more integrated fundraising organization, raising money in our community remains a challenge. In part, we are victims of our own success. Because of Maricopa County's long run of economic expansion and growth, we had abundant resources and the ability to grow dramatically and do a great deal while keeping tuition low. In 2004 the voters overwhelmingly approved the sale of nearly $1 billion in general obligation bonds for buildings and technology. We were never at the top of anyone's

mind where philanthropy was concerned. And although circumstances have changed and we have made progress, more work remains to be done to get people to think of us as a high priority for their philanthropic dollars.

Reflection

The opportunity to write this piece has also provided me an opportunity for reflection. It is clear that fundraising is going to be the new normal at the Maricopa Community Colleges—and for all community colleges. This was not the case a decade ago. After nearly 30 years in the community college world, though, if there is one thing I've come to know it is that the only constant is change. So today fundraising is a priority for me, for our 10 presidents and for our district. But the return on investment of our time comes from so much more than the dollars raised. When I am out talking to a donor, the focus of the conversation is simple: Where are our mutual interests, and what can each of us do to advance those interests? I invest the time and make the effort. Raising the money is important, but the cementing of existing relationships, the creation of new relationships and the opportunity to have others better know our story is of significant importance.

As for any CEO, the demands on my time are significant and the number of hours in the week are finite. Something has had to give. Externally, I've had to pull back from some other commitments and get better at saying no to some of the things that I'm asked to do. Internally, I've had to accept—and, more important, get others to accept—that there are things that don't have to be done by the chancellor, but can be done by others. I don't have to be at every gathering, be part of every discussion and give every welcome. In truth, this helps further develop other leaders and new talent, and it is good both for me, as it helps with balance, and for our district. I continue to encourage our presidents to do the same thing on their campuses.

Finally, I would like to think that our expanding commitment to fundraising, the ongoing change to our culture that this commitment requires and my growing role as a fundraiser are signs of institutional maturity. On the one hand, at 50 years old, we—like so many community colleges around the United States—are still young in comparison to many public and private colleges and universities. On the other hand, we are an institution that is known, recognized and respected across our community and beyond. Our colleges have educated three generations of students and, in some cases, more. We are essential to our community's economic, civic, cultural, and social health and well-being, and we are here to stay. That means that we can and should be an important "top of mind" destination for philanthropic dollars. We want and will do more, do things differently and do things better—for the success of our students.

Chapter 6

NAVIGATING THE RELATIONSHIP BETWEEN GOVERNING AND FOUNDATION BOARDS

By Karen A. Stout

Successful community college fundraising rightfully includes talk about important items like alumni engagement, capital campaigns, annual giving, and the building and development of fundraising teams. We rarely talk about the importance and complexity of the president's need to successfully and deeply engage both the college's governing board and the foundation board of directors—as independent entities, but also as a cohesive and well-aligned executive fundraising team. The strategy of dual engagement of these boards is more art and nuance than science—especially at community colleges, given the local natures of these boards and the reality that private fundraising is still an emerging activity on many community college campuses.

Many community college presidents learn to navigate the two boards on the job. Strategies and tactics for effective leadership of both boards are rarely taught in presidential leadership training programs. Community college governing boards and fundraising boards come in so many shapes and sizes, and with so many different expectations of roles, that it is hard to develop standards of best practice.

Many new presidents come into their positions with little understanding of the anatomy of private fundraising. And even more new presidents, unless they advanced through the development ranks, understand the traditional roles and responsibilities of foundation boards and the complex operational relationships between the foundations and their colleges. For example, according to David Bass and James Lanier, new presidents often do not fully understand an important reality: The college does not control assets donated to the foundation in support of the college ("What Lies Ahead for University-Foundation Relations?" *Association of Governing Boards Magazine,* November/December 2008, p. 19).

With the changing landscape in funding for community colleges (that is, more dependency on tuition revenue and private giving than on public appropriations), navigating the relationship between the two boards will be even more essential to presidential and institutional success. According to Bass and Lanier, "the growth of assets held by foundations, and foundations' increased importance to their affiliated institutions have fostered tensions between institutional and foundation leadership" (p. 15). Many of us have seen these tensions play out on our campuses. Managing these tensions can make or break a presidency or a significant private fundraising program.

Over my community college career, I have worked with four community college foundation boards and four boards of trustees. In three of these experiences, I led the work of the foundation as a development director or advancement vice president. In my current role, as president, I am working with both boards and am actively immersed in navigating the tensions. As a development leader, I watched and supported presidents in navigating the tensions.

Leading both boards along a cohesive pathway can be a challenge, given the distinctive roles and (often political) appointment processes of each board and the resulting composition, individual talents, and individual and collective goals of the respective members. In this chapter I offer some strategies and advice, based on my experiences as both a president and a development leader, to successfully navigate the relationship between the two boards to position community colleges for private fundraising success. The long-term payoff from this dual engagement and relationship building is hard to measure year-to-year, but the engagement is important. Often the success of this work will have its greatest benefit 10, 15 or 20 years from now. This engagement creates a culture of collaboration that has exponential benefits.

The foundations I have worked with are of varying sizes at community colleges in urban, suburban and metropolitan settings, with enrollments ranging from 4,000 to 22,000 students. Montgomery County Community College, located in metropolitan Philadelphia, has had a foundation in place since 1983, but the college was mostly passive in private fundraising until the past six years. When I arrived at the college, I focused on building our public grants capacity, growing public grants revenue from $800,000 annually to more than $10 million annually. The foundation has grown systematically with attention to annual giving, alumni development, major gifts and planned giving; it now raises about $2 million per year. We are in the middle of our first comprehensive capital campaign, to raise about $10 million for scholarships and—more important—to establish a culture of philanthropy that the college can build on for decades.

Clarifying roles: Who does what?

Tension can arise when there is lack of clarity around the degree of independence or separateness of the foundation from the college, when there is lack of agreement on expectations regarding costs of operating the foundation, when there are few agreed-upon metrics to evaluate the success of the foundation's work, and when one board is perceived to have more influence or control than another over fundraising priorities and contributions to fundraising.

When I facilitate conversations between foundation boards and trustees, I often start with a useful tool, a "Who does what?" exercise. I ask each individual to complete a "Who does what?" assessment, and then I break the group into small teams with cross-functional membership and ask the team to reach consensus on each function or role. The exercise sparks a lot of conversation, some laughter and some tense moments. Although there are some basic best practices in who does what, some answers will vary based on institutional context and history, and the maturity and recent success of the institution's fundraising efforts. What is most important is to gain clarity across the two boards on who is responsible for leading and implementing the core fundraising functions: the college's governing board, the foundation board or the development staff (knowing that, in some functional areas, there could be joint accountabilities).

At Montgomery County Community College, the roles of members on the respective boards are clearly outlined and articulated in orientation and planning sessions.

For instance, the board of trustees

- sets policy for the college;
- authorizes the formation of the foundation and makes careful provisions for its liaison and control;
- sets fundraising priorities, public and private, through endorsement of the college's strategic plan and annual operating goals to advance that plan;
- translates funding priorities into specific parameters for private fundraising needs;
- ratifies the appointment of foundation personnel (since these are college employees) and determines the compensation and evaluation of these personnel; and
- ratifies the foundation's annual and long-range fundraising goals.

The foundation board

- sets policy and determines action plans for the foundation;
- provides financial support;
- identifies prospective donors and cultivates and stewards their interests and engagement with the college;
- stewards foundation funds, including overseeing annual audits, setting annual budgets, monitoring expenses and overseeing the investment of funds;
- acts as an ambassador and promotes the college in the community; and
- asks for contributions from prospective donors.

In addition, the development of job descriptions can be used to codify the clarity that emerges from this exercise. Our foundation board members have clear job descriptions with specific fundraising responsibilities that include, among other activities,

- making personal contributions at a level that demonstrates significant dedication to the future of the college;
- reviewing and approving the foundation budget;
- being involved in the identification, cultivation and solicitation of major prospects, including alumni, other individuals, foundations and corporations, preparing them for a significant gift;
- bringing the names of five prospects for gifts of $10,000 or more; and
- hosting or facilitating one or two small cultivation gatherings.

Each year the foundation board does a self-assessment, evaluating their collective and individual performance against the expectations articulated in their job descriptions. The process and the results of this assessment offer an excellent opportunity to hold frank conversations with high and low contributors from the board.

The trustees' roles and responsibilities related to private fundraising are articulated clearly in the trustees' handbook, and the board orientation program includes a component about the linkage of the governing board with the foundation board and private fundraising. The governing board chair—not the president—holds other trustees accountable for this aspect of their job. Given the president's role in stewarding donors, a strong relationship with the governing board chair is essential.

Giving is a stated requirement for members of both groups. For trustees, although many give at leadership levels, the emphasis is on full participation. Again, the governing board chair plays a vital role in advocating for 100 percent giving from the trustees.

Formalizing board linkages

The by-laws of both groups provide a formal way to differentiate and codify their respective roles and responsibilities. The foundation by-laws should include a clear purpose statement that explains how the work of the foundation advances the work of the college. Montgomery's purpose statement makes it clear that the foundation raises dollars only to support advancement of the college's mission:

> "The Foundation shall be operated exclusively for the purpose of providing support and assistance to Montgomery County Community College (hereinafter referred to as the 'College') in developing the programs, facilities and services necessary to carry out the educational mission and functions of the College."

Though simple, the codification of this role is important and has helped to focus efforts of both boards when murky or potentially political fundraising ideas or issues arise.

The foundation by-laws also offer an opportunity to build a bridge between the two boards with an interlocking membership philosophy. At Montgomery, the foundation by-laws call for the college's president to be a voting member of the foundation board.

In addition, the by-laws allow the board of trustee chair to designate one member of the board of trustees as a voting member to the foundation board and for that member to serve in an ex officio role with the foundation board. This call for interlocking membership ensures that the governing board has strong and direct connections with the operations of the foundation board.

The board of trustees' policy infrastructure offers another opportunity to formalize the relationship. Montgomery's board of trustees' handbook includes a policy called "State of Relationship: Montgomery County Community College Foundation and Montgomery County Community College" (Policy 5.9, adopted May 2005). The policy outlines the purpose of the foundation; states that private fundraising priorities must be aligned with the fulfillment of the college's strategic plan; notes that all private gifts to the college should be received, credited and acknowledged by the foundation; and, because the foundation is technically a component unit of the college's audit, clarifies that the foundation must undergo an annual audit of "sufficient excellence to be placed alongside that of the college without disclaimer." The policy also states that the foundation is to assume a portion of the overhead costs associated with operation of the foundation at an amount to be determined annually.

The fiscal relationship

An area of underlying but often immediate tension is the lack of clarity around the fiscal relationship between the college and the foundation. As alluded to in Montgomery's "State of Relationship" policy, core questions are, How is self-sufficiency determined or defined? What should the college contribute to the foundation's operations? How and when should assets be transferred? An agreement, usually a memorandum of understanding, should identify who pays for what, including

- professional staff and benefits;
- support staff and benefits;
- hardware and software;
- staff travel and professional development;
- office space;
- marketing and material development support; and
- financial services support (audit, liability insurance, investment management services).

Answers will vary from college to college, although, due to their relatively small size and modest endowments, most community college foundations are funded largely by their respective college or district. What matters most is that both boards answer and revisit these questions regularly. Presidential leadership and facilitation of these conversations is critical.

At Montgomery, the college supports nearly all of the foundation's expenses, except for some marketing and materials, and provides financial services support such as the audit, liability insurance and investment management services. With the foundation facing limited flexibility in raising unrestricted gifts and the college facing cuts in public funding, these fiscal relationship pressures are ever present and increasing.

The strategic plan drives alignment

A college's strategic plan is really a case statement for public and private funding, and it offers a perfect road map to align private fundraising priorities and opportunities. Montgomery's strategic plan to 2016, "Beyond Access," has six strategic goals with corresponding "critical success factors." Cascading out of the strategic plan are several auxiliary plans including a facilities master plan and an academic program plan. The diagram below shows how fundraising priorities align with four components of the college's strategic plan:

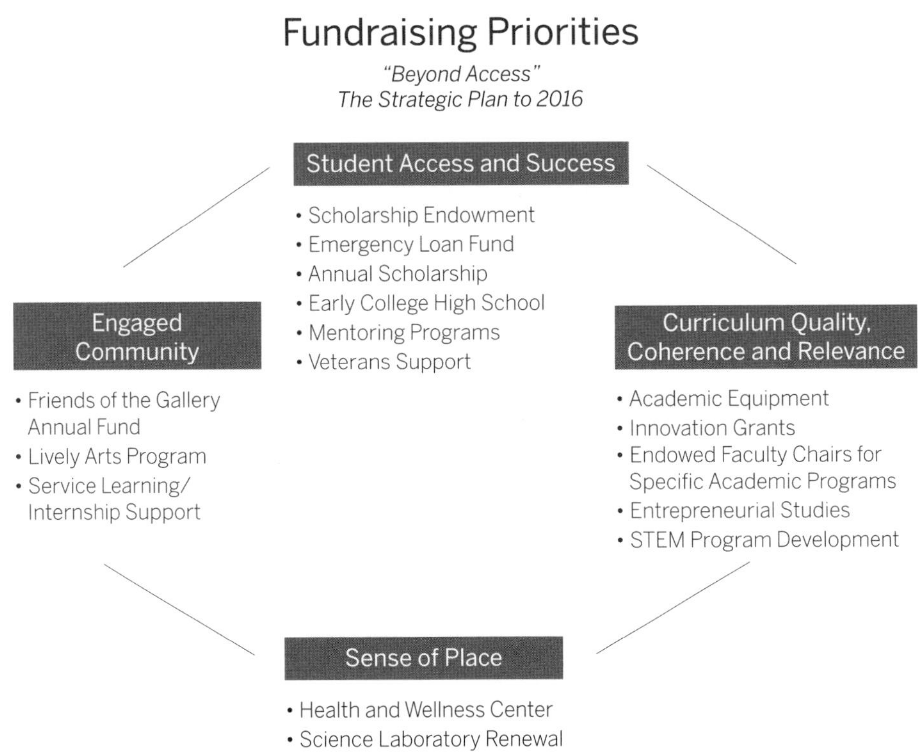

Scholarship support and private giving for our early college high school efforts clearly advance the college's student access and success goals. Specific support for academic program development, faculty development, and academic equipment advances the goal of ensuring program relevancy. Capital support for facilities outlined in the facilities master plan advances the sense of place goal. Private support for our art galleries, civic engagement opportunities for students and the Lively Arts series supports our goal to build an engaged community.

Ideas for funding that fall outside this framework are not advanced for consideration. Over the years, I have found this diagram to be useful in shaping planning priorities with the foundation board, in working with donors and in ensuring that foundation staff stay focused.

While the board of trustees ultimately endorses the final strategic, facilities master, and academic plans, the foundation board has a consultative role, as a stakeholder in the process, in the development of the final draft plans. Thus both boards have buy-in for the fundraising priorities and, as a result, alignment around a sense of purpose.

Informal mechanisms for collaboration

Perhaps the most powerful tools for building alignment across the two groups are informal. These informal linkages can include regular reports of the boards' activities to each other. For example, on a quarterly basis, the Montgomery trustee with interlocking membership responsibilities updates colleague trustees on the work of the foundation board.

My monthly president's report to the board of trustees does the same thing. I also offer a president's report at the quarterly meetings of the foundation board so that they are aware of college-based issues.

Special social activities, especially those designed for donor cultivation or recognition of scholarship recipients, offer unique opportunities for members of each board and their spouses or partners to engage in a low-stress setting. Our Salute to Excellence event is a "don't miss" event for both boards. Though sponsored by the foundation to honor donors and students, the trustees have a strong role at the event in a pre-reception for donors and with a formal role for the board chair in the event program. Joint dinner meetings with limited and focused agendas can also be powerful in bringing together the leadership groups of both boards.

A thought about alumni boards

Many community colleges started with alumni boards before they built foundation boards. In some cases, both boards still exist. In these cases, it is important not to create or encourage two competing fundraising organizations. It should be clear that the alumni board is not a fundraising board. Of course, fundraising, in partnership with the foundation, should be a role the alumni board advances or endorses. This chapter has focused on the relationship between the governing and foundation boards, but the alumni board or council must also be engaged by the president and aligned with the work of these boards. Alumni leaders are a good source of talent—a farm team—for potential foundation directors and trustees. Connecting the alumni board members with the trustees and foundation directors builds awareness of the pipeline of talent.

Most of these connections are informal, but they include

- regularly recognizing alumni board members at events as VIP attendees;
- showcasing alumni board members with speaking roles at high-impact events;
- engaging alumni board members on fundraising committees, including annual giving; and
- designing and delivering at least one high-impact alumni-led event annually that also acts as a donor development and cultivation event (our annual Alumni Hall of Fame event has a popular following).

A thought about leadership development

In the recently released brief *American Association of Community Colleges Competencies for Community College Leaders* (2013), private fundraising proficiency is noted as an important competency for new and seasoned presidents. Specifically, the competencies include a need to "learn the skills necessary to lead a foundation board" (p. 8). With a significant number of presidents set to retire in the coming years, and with the already-high turnover in the development profession, it is important to include training in this area of dual board engagement and management in leadership development programs—not just for new presidents, but for those in our colleges who aspire to move into vice presidential roles. Turnover in the president or the chief development officer can undo progress made in alignment of the boards unless new presidents and new development officers understand the context and the questions to be asked on arrival at a new institution.

Turnover in board of trustee leadership or significant turnover in board of trustee membership, which can also happen suddenly and abruptly, can be just as damaging. Thus it is also important for organizations like the Association of Community College Trustees to include in their development programs some training for trustees around their governance role in supporting a successful foundation and private fundraising agenda.

When training trustees and others on these topics, I often use case studies involving fundraising efforts gone awry as tools for helping them to understand the importance of managing the potential tension between the college and the foundation.

Closing thought

In navigating the relationship between the two boards, the president must build an environment of mutual respect, trust, accountability and transparency. This requires continual facilitation of difficult conversations (e.g., the "Who does what?" exercise), the adoption and use of formal tools and processes like clear by-laws and strong policy infrastructures, a strong and compelling strategic plan that operationalizes alignment of purpose, and design and leadership of informal activities that build spirit and collaboration across the boards.

I find the best way to align this relationship-building work (and maintain my own sanity and spirit!) is to leverage the power of student stories. Students, whose grit and persistence is often humbling, have an uncanny way of helping us to navigate the tensions, which disperse immediately when they are placed rightly in the center of our work.

Chapter 7

DO YOU HAVE THE FOUNDATION BOARD YOU WANT? DO YOU WANT THE BOARD YOU HAVE?

By E. Ann McGee

As someone who aspired to be a president, I knew many years ago that I was missing a key credential—fundraising. That's what motivated me to take a position as vice president for development at a large community college in the South.

What I didn't know was that the college's foundation, one of the oldest in the nation, had assets of only $800,000 and debt of over $1 million for a piece of property they had accepted. They also had a foundation board that was composed of 30 community leaders—most of whom were there just because they wanted to support the college president and be at the periodic breakfasts with him. They had never really been asked to raise any money or be advocates for the college.

It was the classic old-school model for foundation boards. Unfortunately, to varying degrees, it's a model that many presidents inherit. A high-performing foundation board is essential to achieving a president's vision, so here's my experience and some advice on transforming your volunteer fundraisers.

Board assessment

When you became president of your first institution, what did you find in terms of the composition and track record of the foundation board that you inherited? My experience as the vice president for development was enlightening and also somewhat frightening. What I found was a group of 30 powerful individuals who had never been encouraged or taught how to fundraise for the college. One of the first tasks the president assigned to me was to meet with each board member and ask if he or she wanted to remain on the board. It was my job to assess the members' level of interest both in serving and in *giving* to the college.

As I progressed through these private meetings, I was amazed at what I found. About half of them told me that the college was not a personal priority. They were on the board because they liked the president and wanted to support him. But when it came to giving money, they had other charities and causes that took precedence. When I mentioned making a $1,000 annual gift to the college as a criterion for board membership, at least half of them declined. Needless to say, my report back to the president was not positive. It was at that point that I learned the value of recognizing the contributions that these 30 individuals *had* made to the college over the years. We decided to form a new category of board membership—director emeritus—and invited each board member to select the type of membership that met his or her personal goals. We continued to list these members on the foundation letterhead and invited them to events, but they had earned a new emeritus status.

Years later, in what would become the largest gift that the college had received to date—$9 million—I learned the value of respecting someone's personal goals. To my great surprise, one of the emeritus directors was an attorney who suggested to his dying client that he leave a third of his estate to the college, resulting in the $9 million gift. It certainly made me question what would have happened if we hadn't honored those emeritus directors. What if we had just eliminated them from our roster? Would that significant gift have occurred? It was a great lesson in making sure that people feel good about their contact with your organization. And it is one of the reasons that fundraising is so addictive. You never know what might happen!

So, in your assessment of the foundation board that you inherited, what have you found? Do they represent the "bench strength" that you would like to have, or do you need to find another role for some of them? My first "ask" of you would be to complete an assessment of your board and determine if they will get you where you want to go. If not, what is the most appropriate way to honor their commitment to the college and move on?

Board composition

In leaving the college where I was the development vice president and moving into the presidency at Seminole State College of Florida, I was amazed to find that Seminole had a board that was similar to the original one at my previous institution. They had raised very little money, but there was an added twist. Seminole's foundation board was composed of only five college employees. These were certainly not the people who had the influence and clout to attract significant dollars to the institution.

So, at Seminole, the goal was to hire a dynamic executive director for the foundation and set about identifying key leaders in the community who had an interest in the college—or could be persuaded to develop a keen interest in the college. As a new president, my joke was that I had given "120 speeches in 120 days." That wasn't far from the truth, as my predecessor had been dealing with health issues during his last 10 years and hadn't been active in the community. The community was hungry to learn about the college, and the personal appearances were a great opportunity for me to "scout" for potential foundation members.

It didn't take long to identify one particular individual who seemed to know everyone in the community and was a great "connector" for people and projects. I asked him to be our first foundation chairman, and he agreed. We then developed criteria for board membership and assessed the people and industries that needed to be represented as we moved the college ahead.

Each community has a unique identity with different criteria for the "power brokers." You know the difference that your college makes in your community. Who are the people or companies that benefit? Should they be associated with you? How do you attract them? There will be a different set of answers for each college, but some of the questions you might ask include the following:

- Do you want your foundation board to be a "destination board" in your community? In other words, do you want your board to be viewed as one of the most influential in your community?
- Do you want primarily CEOs serving on your board? Peers give to peers. Is it possible to have a mix of executives on your board, or do you need to keep it a high-level membership so that you can attract the people that have the most impact?
- Does your board membership mirror your community in terms of demographics? Does it matter? How do you achieve the involvement of your entire community so that everyone feels represented?
- Does the mix of board membership represent the key industries in your community?
- Is geography important? Are all the physical sectors of your service area included?
- Is there a population or segment of your business community that has been overlooked or forgotten in assembling your board? In other words, who is at the table, and who is missing?

Board recruitment

In his book *Good to Great* (HarperCollins, 2001), Jim Collins writes about "getting the right people on the bus." That principle is definitely fundamental as you assemble those who are going to help advance the college's mission and raise funds to support your priorities. So, who should you look for? What qualities should they possess? Do they need a knowledge base about your institution, or can they be fresh recruits?

Recruitment is a year-round, never-ending process. You and those associated with your foundation and college should always be searching for individuals who would make great board members. With that said, do you have opportunities so that a potential board member could experience the college prior to membership? Are there advisory committees that might serve as a natural training ground? Are there key industries that should be represented by virtue of their interest in your training programs? The potential for productive board members is truly endless.

Many years ago, we formed an annual giving club called simply the "President's Club." It requires a $1,000 annual gift and involves three breakfast meetings a year. These breakfasts serve as a business networking opportunity for President's Club members while providing a forum to showcase our faculty and student successes. Through the President's Club events, we have been able to identify business leaders and educate them about the college. You might consider this as a "bullpen" of sorts for the foundation board. What are the natural opportunities at your college where someone might get involved and learn more about the college while also being subtly auditioned for board membership? Every interaction that you have provides the opportunity to recruit someone to your cause.

Besides the community members that you recruit for your board, what about looking internally? Over the years, we have found that the active involvement of faculty and trustees can be critical in generating both support and understanding for the foundation's role at the college. Each year, the Faculty Senate is asked to nominate one member from its ranks as a foundation board member. We ask the same of the board of trustees. We have found that the faculty members who serve have a deeper understanding of the support that the college enjoys from the community—and why it is important. They have become champions among the faculty and have helped us increase our annual employee giving program. Many of them also become active contributors to the foundation—giving of their own wealth—such as an endowed teaching chair—or connecting the foundation with business leaders who employ their students and program graduates. The possibilities are limitless.

Trustee membership on the foundation board has been a great way to keep the entire board of trustees connected to the foundation's goals. It is a way to make sure that the two groups' efforts are coordinated and understood. The designated trustee is responsible for making monthly reports to the trustees at their meeting and for making the quarterly reports at the foundation meetings. The goal is to both increase understanding between the groups and make sure that the foundation is aligning its fundraising with the college's identified goals.

Board expectations

In recruiting potential board members, make sure they know what is required of them. They need to know—up front—that you are expecting them to bring "time, talent and treasure" to the organization. Applying the adage "give, get, or get off" is fair only if the person knows what is expected before he or she joins your organization. You might want to prepare an official document to give to potential members, but we had a board chair who summed up the criteria succinctly. He told our board members that they needed to advocate, serve, participate, donate and show up! He then gave each of them a small gift. It was a shovel that was positioned halfway into the metal grounding piece that served as the base for the memento. On the base were the words "Dig Deeper." It was his personal challenge to them to dig deeper into their pockets, into their relationship base and into their contact potential so that they could make an even greater difference for the college.

None of us had known that the board chair was going to take such a personal interest and be so creative, but it certainly worked. Everyone left that board meeting with a physical reminder of their promise made on behalf of our students. The shovels served as conversation starters when people visited their offices. And it was a great way for the chair to follow up with each board member when he asked them to dig deeper for the college.

In reflecting on my days as a development officer, I remember the discussion that the board had when they adopted the membership criteria. There was considerable discussion about requiring a financial commitment, about meeting attendance, about committee service and about members' roles as advocates for the college. In the end, we had the entire board adopt the membership criteria. It wasn't determined by the college leadership. It was something that the board determined was appropriate for themselves as members and was in the best interest of the college. Today, we require a board member either to give $1,000 annually from their personal or company resources or to raise $5,000. They must attend three of four board meetings per year. We publish the attendance record with each board agenda packet as a visual reminder. They are also required to serve on at least one committee. Of course, extenuating circumstances do arise, but there can be no misunderstanding about their commitment to us, and vice versa.

Board training and socialization

Presidents tend to assume that our constituents know how good our institutions are and how valuable we are to our communities. In nearly two decades as president, I have come to understand that we aren't understood. We know our graduation rates, average starting salaries, how many students transfer to the universities and how many of the local high school students we enroll. But the average person in our community truly doesn't know the real impact we have on the economic well-being of our communities.

Your foundation board members are charged with being your advocates, but they can be effective in that role only if you educate them and continue to reeducate them. We have used our board meetings as an opportunity to feature student and faculty speakers who always foster the "wow" factor in the board members. The students' experiences and the hurdles that they overcome just to be students are truly amazing. Hearing a presentation by one of our faculty members always reinforces that our faculty are truly masters at teaching and at nurturing students. But what are some other opportunities to educate and involve board members? How about graduation? Convocation? Serving on college committees?

One of the best "education" experiences that our foundation has hosted for both board members and faculty is the awarding of endowed teaching chairs. Faculty compete for these cash awards, and the final selection is made by a foundation board committee that interviews these master teachers and participates in a practice classroom experience. Needless to say, once a business leader is a "student" in the presence of these incredibly motivated and passionate faculty, they want to award each one of them an endowed teaching chair. At the same time, the faculty gain a new appreciation for the caliber of the business and community leaders who are actively generating financial support for them. It is truly a win-win situation and a great way to educate both groups about the power and commitment each has made to the college.

Another opportunity for interaction and education is in the competition for foundation mini-grants. Every year the foundation awards about $40,000 in mini-grants. Every employee at the college can apply for a grant that averages $2,000. In reading the grant proposals, the foundation committee acquires an in-depth knowledge of the programming needs at the college. Committee members also see the impact that even a small grant can make. In some cases, because of their knowledge of our community, they are able to suggest partnerships that can increase the reach of the college. It is all part of the education process ... and it is a real-world experience for our board members.

But there is more to educating board members than just teaching them about the college. Many of them fear asking people for money. I can well remember a workshop that we held for our foundation board members during which the consultant asked them to raise their hands if they were *not* comfortable asking people for money. The first hand that shot up was a company head who had just raised a million dollars for us to expand some of our career programs that provided workers for his industry. I was shocked when he raised his hand and questioned him. His response was, "I can do it. But that doesn't mean that I *like* doing it."

The consultant had a great response for our board members. He asked them if they would be willing to invite someone to lunch and talk about the college. Or would they be willing to host a cocktail party in their home and talk about the college. He helped them to understand that we first and foremost needed them as our advocates. College personnel could close the deal. We just needed them to help make the ask as successful as possible.

We also have started providing our board members with wallet cards that have five key facts about the college. We equip them with a short elevator speech. We send them YouTube videos featuring real students. We ask the student scholarship winners to write thank you notes to our foundation board members, and we ask the board members to write thank you notes to major donors. It is all part of the education process that is ongoing and personal.

Another important element of board education is socialization. Since this group will interact with each other on a limited basis throughout the year, it is important to provide a way for them to socialize and have fun with each other. Even as we talk about the importance of students connecting with the institution so that they will persist, we need to make sure that our board members and their spouses also connect with each other. You might want to partner a seasoned board member with a newly appointed board member. Hosting a cocktail hour following a board meeting, a special event in your planetarium or some other facility that you want to showcase, or a golf tournament are all ways to increase personal interaction. Creating meaningful situations that help board members get to know each other and connect on both a personal and a professional level will definitely increase their commitment to the college. They are there to help you, but they are also there to increase their sphere of influence. Plus, life is too short not to have fun!

Board accountability, evaluation and rotation

Even as trustee boards complete annual self-assessments, foundation boards will find that this is a good way to assess their accomplishments over the year and their progress toward their established goals. Board members should be encouraged to complete an annual self-assessment that might include questions such as

- Do I know and support the organization's mission and purpose?
- Have I supported the chief executive and reviewed his or her performance?
- Have I been part of effective organizational planning?
- Have I ensured that adequate resources are available for the organization?
- Have I helped to effectively manage the organization's resources?
- Have I helped to determine, monitor and strengthen the organization's programs and services?
- Have I enhanced the organization's public standing?
- Have I ensured the accountability of the organization, both legally and ethically?
- Have I actively recruited new board members?
- What benefits have I gained by serving on this board?
- What have been my concerns or frustrations?
- What strengths did I bring to the board, and how would I rate my performance?
- Do I continue to have the energy, time and commitment needed to serve on this board?

An annual "checkup" will help board members to focus on the scope of their responsibility and how they have contributed individually to the organization's success. You could also include questions related to specific behaviors that were expected of board members, such as

- Did I contact 10 prospects during the year?
- Did I call donors to thank them for their gifts?
- Did I drop a personal note to lapsed donors?
- Did I identify prospects and get them to attend cultivation events?
- Did I donate at my top level?
- Did I identify and recruit future board members?
- Did I speak frequently about the college, its programs and its purposes?
- Did I accompany staff on cultivation and solicitation visits?

Once a board member has served for the specified number of years, it is important that you exercise board rotation. Yes, you can wear out even your staunchest supporters. Whether it is a three-year, six-year or longer term, you can provide for a one-year "sabbatical" and then invite the person to return to the board.

Conclusion

I do not believe that an institution can be successful at fundraising without a powerful, knowledgeable and connected foundation board—a group that is viewed and treated as a valued partner. To that end, you should select wisely, educate appropriately, set achievable goals and periodically assess and celebrate their success. By involving educated and dedicated board members, we can significantly increase our opportunities to advance and enhance the economic well-being of our regions. We are truly all in this together!

The goal is to personalize the experience on the foundation board so that all members realize that this is their commitment, their community, their legacy.

Bibliography

Collins, Jim. (2001). *Good to Great: Why Some Companies Make the Leap ... and Others Don't.* New York: HarperCollins.

Loring, Chuck V. (2009, March). *Getting Governance Right: Building a Strong Nonprofit Board for Responsible Governance.* Workshop presented at a meeting of the Foundation for Seminole State College Board of Directors, Sanford, FL.

Milliron, Mark David, de los Santos, Gerardo E., & Browning, Boo. (Eds.). (2004). *Successful Approaches to Fundraising and Development (New Directions for Community Colleges, No. 124).* San Francisco, CA: Jossey-Bass.

Mott, William R. (2012). *The Board Game: A Story of Hope and Inspiration for CEOs and Governing Boards.* Publisher: William R. Mott.

Sprinkel Grace, Kay. (2005). *The Ultimate Board Member's Book—A 1-Hour Guide to Understanding and Fulfilling Your Role and Responsibilities.* Medfield, MA: Emerson & Church.

Section III

FUNDRAISING

Chapter 8

ASSESSING THE RELATIONSHIP WITH YOUR CHIEF FUNDRAISER

By Rae Goldsmith

For community colleges looking to improve their fundraising, here's one key piece of advice: Mind the gap.

Which gap? The communications and perceptions gap between the college chief executive and the chief development officer that, if not tended to, can threaten working relationships, derail careers and jeopardize fundraising success.

In 2012 the Council for Advancement and Support of Education (CASE) surveyed community college presidents and chief development officers to compare perspectives about fundraising and their respective roles in the process. The results were encouraging—and instructive.

CASE received responses from 70 chief executives (CEOs) and 137 chief development officers (CDOs). The respondents were not necessarily CEO/CDO pairs from the same colleges or districts.

Although the results are important, especially as we were able to draw correlations, the questions themselves should serve as a useful tool for any pair of leaders working together to increase private support to their institution.

The CEO/CDO relationship

Fortunately, there was widespread agreement to the fundamental question of whether the CEO and CDO have an effective working relationship. More than three-quarters of the CEOs and CDOs agreed or strongly agreed.

When asked if the CDO uses the CEO's time effectively, there was a strong positive response—and only a slight gap. Seventy-two percent of CEOs agreed or strongly agreed, compared with 76 percent of CDOs. In other words, there was a relatively modest 4-percentage-point difference—or gap in perception—between the two groups.

Another important element in the working relationship is how well the CDO prepares the CEO for donor visits. Here the perception gap widened a bit, with not as many CEOs as CDOs in the "agree" or "strongly agree" camp. However, once again the responses were overwhelmingly positive, with the majority of both groups believing that the CEO was indeed well prepared by the CDO.

Perhaps one of the more challenging roles for the development officer is helping the president improve his or her fundraising skills. Frankly, it can be tough to mentor the boss. Not surprisingly, then, there were lower levels of agreement and a widening gap between the two groups. It is quite possible that CEOs don't feel they need improvement or that they don't expect the CDO to play this role. Yet many presidents can benefit from coaching.

The survey also asked how often the two colleagues meet. Surprisingly, there was a significant gap between the responses of the two groups. While 39 percent of CEOs said they meet at least once a day, only 22 percent of CDOs gave the same answer. The gap was even wider—32 percentage points—if you combine the answers for "at least once a day" and "about once a day." It may simply be that it feels to presidents like those development officers are after them all the time.

Does the CEO understand the fundraising process? Nearly 90 percent of responding presidents agreed or strongly agreed that they do, while only 63 percent of development officers held that view about their presidents. That yields a significant perception gap of 26 percentage points. As suggested earlier, presidential self-confidence might make it difficult for the development officer to coach the boss.

A similar perception gap exists between the president and the fundraiser regarding the president's comfort level with asking for a gift. And while the size of the gap is roughly the same as the gap for presidential understanding of the fundraising process, both groups were less likely to agree that the president is comfortable asking for a gift. This too could be a useful entry point for a conversation between the development officer and the president about effective techniques. The development officer should enter this conversation recognizing that most presidents don't come to their positions with a lot of experience in working with donors.

Along these same lines, development officers are less positive than presidents in their views regarding the CEO's role in actively cultivating donors for a gift.

When it comes to stewarding donors after the gift, the perception gap narrows a bit, as the agreement level in both groups decreases. Sixty-eight percent of CEOs agreed or strongly agreed that they actively steward donors, compared with 59 percent of CDOs. The reasons that someone might not agree with a statement may be perfectly understandable. In this case, the CEO and the CDO may have agreed that the best use of the president's time would be in cultivation rather than in stewardship.

Expectations

In a few cases the results fall in the negative range. Fewer than 50 percent of both groups agreed or strongly agreed that the CEO spends an appropriate amount of time on fundraising. Clearly there is some level of concern and frustration around this point.

How much time does the CEO spend on fundraising? Generally presidents feel they spend more time on it than do the development officers. Both groups suggest it is rare for the president to spend more than 50 percent of his or her time on fundraising activities. Half of the development officers place the amount of time at less than 10 percent.

Are fundraising goals realistic? CEOs generally agreed that their institutions' goals were realistic (71 percent); CDOs, not so much (53 percent). The 18-percentage-point gap between the two is reason for some conversation if not some concern. And it is certainly of concern that nearly half of the CDOs did not view goals as realistic.

Regardless, does the CDO have the resources he or she needs to achieve the institution's fundraising goals? Here we saw the lowest agreement level among development officers and one of the largest perception gaps of any in the survey. Fewer than one quarter of the fundraisers said the college is investing adequately in the advancement program; more than half of the presidents believed that to be the case. (That said, there likely are very few institutions—two-year or four-year—that invest in their fundraising programs at levels that would enable them to fully reach their potential.)

Boards and roles

The survey also looked at the roles of governing boards and affiliated foundation boards in the fundraising operation. We wanted to get some sense of the working relationships among boards, presidents and development officers.

For example, we wanted to know if the chief fundraiser is considered a member of the college's senior management team. Roughly two-thirds of both CEOs and CDOs agreed that the chief fundraiser is a member of the president's or chancellor's cabinet.

When asked if the CEO actively engages the board of the affiliated foundation, roughly two-thirds of presidents and half of development officers agreed. That's a notable gap of 15 percentage points.

Perhaps a bit more disturbing is that less than half of the development officers agreed that the foundation board and the governing board have a shared mission and vision. Presidents, however, were much more optimistic on this point. Shared mission and vision may be a healthy starting point for conversation, as it will be difficult to significantly advance fundraising efforts without strong alignment between these two key entities.

We found the single greatest perception gap on perceptions about the fundraiser-in-chief. When asked whether the president is the college's or district's chief fundraiser, 79 percent of presidents agreed, compared with just 44 percent of fundraisers. The perception gap of 35 percentage points is the largest among all the survey questions. Some of this gap might be attributed to differing interpretations of the question. However, there should be no question that, while the development officer is the professional staff person responsible for managing the fundraising operation, the president is the person whose vision, integrity, connections and presence are essential to securing most major gifts for the college.

Success factors

CASE research staff analyzed responses to individual survey questions to see what clues they provide about factors that contribute to fundraising success. (Although there are some strong correlations, remember that multiple factors contribute to an institution's fundraising totals in any given year.)

For example, how does the experience level of presidents and development officers correlate with amount of money raised? There is a correlation, especially among fundraisers. For those running programs that raised at least $1.5 million during the last fiscal year, 70 percent had at least four years of experience.

There is also a correlation between fundraising totals and the number of years a president and fundraiser have worked together. Among schools that raised more than $500,000, more than 40 percent had CEOs and CDOs who had worked together for at least four years. This suggests that an enduring partnership pays dividends.

There appear to be even bigger dividends from the time the CEO spends on fundraising. The CEOs of institutions raising more than $1.5 million are far more likely to be spending more than a quarter of their time on fundraising.

Regular interaction between the CEO and the CDO also correlates with higher fundraising totals. This is especially true for presidents who said they interact at least daily with their development officers.

On a similar point, chief development officers who are raising the most money are much more likely to be members of the president's cabinet, the survey showed. Among other things, this suggests that the opportunity for the CDO to be part of strategic discussions and decisions at the college enhances his or her ability to secure significant gifts for the institution.

Conversation starters

Every working relationship requires care and feeding in order to be successful. What's most important is that presidents and their chief fundraisers talk openly and honestly about what they need, their goals, and how they can continue to forge a strong partnership. A starting point for the conversation may be for the CEO and the CDO to take the

CASE survey individually and compare notes. The survey and other information on the findings can be found on the CASE website at *www.case.org (http://bit.ly/GAPsurvey).*

Another approach might be to start a conversation that identifies and builds on each other's strengths with some positive reinforcement. Share with each other one thing the other does that contributes to the institution's fundraising success. From there, identify one thing the other person can do to improve success.

Presidents, try asking your CDOs the following questions:

- Who are the biggest donors in the last week/month/quarter, and how can I help thank them?
- What do you need from me to cultivate people on your major gift list?
- How did I do on the last donor visit? Suggestions for improvement?
- Where is my time best spent, and where am I not needed?
- Do you feel comfortable telling me what I need to hear, even if I don't want to hear it?
- How are we doing ... really?

Fundraisers, try asking your CEOs these questions:

- Are you getting the fundraising information you want and need, in a manner that works for you?
- How can I make more effective use of your limited time?
- How else can I help you accomplish your goals for the college?
- What are our fundraising goals and priorities?
- How are we doing ... really?

By making questions like these part of regular, open conversation, presidents and chief fundraisers can close the gaps that derail a good working relationship and lay the groundwork for long-term fundraising success.

Chapter 9

THERE'S A FUNDRAISER HIDDEN WITHIN EACH OF US

By Thom D. Chesney

If the news releases for college presidential appointments are accurate, very few community college CEOs come to their jobs with extensive experience in the advancement or foundation office. Even if it's not mentioned in the job description, though, the presidency also comes with another unofficial title: chief fundraising officer. Depending on one's pathway to the presidency, experience in new revenue generation, development and alumni relations may be extensive or slim to none—and is more often the latter.

Fortunately, fundraising entails a set of skills and insights that presidents typically possess on arrival but may not immediately self-identify as transferable. Making a compelling case for increased state and federal funding to a legislative appropriations committee one day is really not much different from delivering a similarly compelling narrative for alumni giving the next. Audiences may change, but both settings emphasize building relationships and shared values. Many skills a president acquires informally in other arenas, from corporate work to social settings, are highly transferrable to fundraising.

The result? There's a fundraiser hidden in each of us.

I like to think of fundraising as a three-legged stool: the message, the audience, and the shared goals of the sender and the receiver. All three are interdependent. If one is weak, the others cannot support the platform that results in fundraising success.

A simple way of looking at this is in the day-to-day conversations we have with colleagues and friends. We're comfortable with these because we have much in common, know the audience well, and say exactly what we want to say and can adjust it without much risk of embarrassment or misunderstanding. We expect the pressure to increase in fundraising conversations, but if we draw on the things that put us at ease in regular conversation, we find they serve us well in fundraising, too.

Because you are the chief executive, your audience will make two assumptions when you meet with them: (1) You are important, and (2) you find them important and want to establish, sustain or grow a relationship. Your title alone creates expectations for your audience, but remember that the most important person in the room is a matter of perspective. You can always adjust your audience's expectations based on what you have to say and how you say it.

For example, in the case of existing donors you have never met, you will want to get to know what their relationship has been with the college. This means more than collecting statistics on how much or how often they have given. It also includes at least a summative biography, their history with the college and, quite possibly, their politics. Someone on your development or communications staff should have this information and be able to brief you. (A Google name search on the way to the meeting is insufficient.) In the case of well-established donors, a lot can be gained just by listening to their stories of why they give and what their expectations are for their giving. They want to know and observe that you are a good listener and that they can trust you, as they have your predecessor. Don't feel like the initial meeting with an established or potential donor is all about the ask.

So, how do you make sure the three-legged stool you construct will support your fundraising goals? Fortunately, on the pathway to the presidency you have filled your toolkit with several transferable skills that will make this part of the job easier, increase your comfort level with fundraising and perhaps even make it enjoyable.

The president as storyteller

Think back for a moment to the interview process that led to your selection as president. At each step you inevitably had to do a lot of storytelling, explaining how you develop strategic plans and budgets and how you would measure the success of the institution. As you responded to questions, you likely told several detailed stories that were keenly familiar to you—how you had helped to redesign curricula and programs so that students could be more successful and graduate on time. How during a difficult budget cycle you found a way to balance the books and make the institution even stronger. How during a period of declining enrollments you restructured the recruitment and admissions process, retained more students and turned the trend around. These stories came to you easily because you had time to contemplate, plan and rehearse them. It doesn't hurt that you lived them as well. Storytelling not only is one of your greatest existing tools but also is essential to successful fundraising. There's no need to alter your style or manner from that which is most natural, comfortable and compelling. If you try to "act presidential," your run the risk of appearing artificial and insincere—not the embodiment of all that is your institution. This leads me to a second tool already at your disposal.

You are the institution

One of the things you recognize early on as a president is that practically everyone—students, faculty, staff and the community—perceives you and your institution as one and the same, 24 hours a day, seven days a week. There will be times when you will dread this, like when you want to go outside to collect the morning newspaper but realize that you must first shower and put on a reasonably matching outfit, just in case even one person were to drive or walk by in the roughly 30 seconds it takes you to walk from your front door to the sidewalk and back. Thankfully, most of the time you will enjoy being the institution. It has its privileges.

A key benefit of this assimilated role is that you will have more access than anyone else to information, aspirations, frustrations and expectations from across the institution, thanks to the inundation of emails, reports, memoranda, newsletters, presentations and marketing materials that you receive almost daily. If you can muster a CNN Headline News understanding of all this, you will be able to talk to anyone about anything just long enough to engage them but not bore them, and frequently that is what successful fundraising is all about. As you prepare to meet with a donor, you will spend significant time gaining a deeper, richer understanding of the need that you are trying to meet through that donor and how and why he or she is the perfect fit, but you will rarely be the only one in the conversation. You may find—and have to become comfortable with the fact—that you are sometimes brought in at the point at which the donor wants to meet with you. You may be the opener, the closer, or both, but you will always be the college. Wear it well.

It's about relationships

The third tool, cultivating relationships, is a skill that likely helped you earn your job as president, and it also plays a key role in fundraising. If you took a traditional pathway like me, you may have launched your career as a faculty member and wound your way through a series of career changes that included department chair and one or more deanships before becoming a chief academic officer. If, along the way, you somehow managed to attain tenure or a multiyear teaching contract, then you also navigated a process mercifully shorter than the Spanish Inquisition but only slightly less painful. Whatever your route, you have already encountered just about every type of audience—individual or group—that you will encounter when you fund raise.

Remember the well-meaning colleague who wanted to know everything you did, how you did it and how often, and was always willing to tell you how you could do it all better? Good news! You will get to meet him again in the form of someone who has a check to write but before he does expects not only that you want to hear every compliment and criticism he has about the college you wear, but also that you will find a way to meet his expectations for and through his donation.

I have found it immensely valuable in these interactions to remember one word: SMILE—Surely Must I Listen Eternally—near the top of my list of favorite presidential acronyms. Reciting this word internally, as a mantra of sorts, always turns the corners of my mouth upward and refocuses my eyes intently on my audience. If you choose to adopt it, I suggest you practice with family and friends who are in on the game and not during a cabinet or board meeting, where you have much more to lose if someone sees through your "SMILE."

The opposite extreme is the silent person who says very little and expects you to fill in the void with just the right words, just the right messaging and in just the right amount of time. In these situations you can quickly begin to feel like you're in an episode of *Shark Tank*, trying to make a pitch to a handful of venture capitalists who at any moment might say, "I'm out," without telling you why, asking any questions or giving you any indication of what went wrong. It is therefore critically important that you read your audience's facial and postural cues and find an intentional moment in which you bring the audience into the conversation. Your pre-meeting preparation will have told you the audience's background and giving history, and from this you can draw in an otherwise silent party into a two-way conversation by saying something like, "This will double the number of nurses we can graduate, helping fill the critical shortage that your company has spotlighted in its strategic priorities. What has been your experience with the nurses you've hired from our program?"

It is not an oversimplification to say that if you cultivate fundraising relationships the way you have your strongest friendships, you will ultimately be more successful. Just as you experience in friendships:

- be willing to listen as often as you share;
- be ready to lead or follow a conversation;
- don't expect every first meeting to lead to a second; and
- don't expect one awkward meeting to be the end of the relationship.

Making your case

Whether you believe persuasion to be an art or skill, it is the fourth tool that you already possess and have likely practiced, and you will need to make the most of it when it comes to fundraising. I believe there's great value in making a note of the times in your life when being persuasive helped you out.

In my own case, a story from third grade recess comes to mind. It was the first week of school and I had transferred from three states away, so it was too early for me to have made any friends. When it was time to go outside to play, I pretty much stood in silence along the wall with a bunch of other boys who didn't much look like they cared to join in football, tetherball or tag either. At some point my stare was broken by a boy who came up and stood directly in front of me. He was ringed by three other boys who appeared to be his entourage—a word I learned much later—and I was smart enough to know that this probably signified that he was the playground bully. All of this was confirmed when he asked, "Are you the new kid?"

No one ever gets asked that except when they are about to get punched. So I think he was surprised when I replied, "Yes, I am. How can I help you?" By the puzzled look on his face, it appeared to me that no one had ever asked him if they could help him, which caught him completely off guard and allowed the silence between us to hang just long enough for the bell to ring and the crowd to disperse. Somehow, offering to help was all it took to start a relationship that, although never warm, never led to blows either. I carry that with me today as a reminder that sometimes the simplest of remarks can be the most persuasive.

Several years later, I would be offered a job as a department manager in a Macy's store in Atlanta. I had just graduated from college with a degree in Spanish and was not entirely sure how my academic preparation plus six weeks of Macy's reprogramming made me qualified to supervise about three dozen women ranging in age from 16 to 60 in the handbags, hosiery, hats and fashion jewelry departments. Fortunately, much as I today let my college do most of the talking, I learned back then to let the merchandise lead while I filled in the blanks. Back then I would have said to a customer, "Do you see how the onyx complements your hair color, and the teardrop shape aligns perfectly with your ear lobe? You'll wear these for years to come." Today with a potential donor, that might translate as something like, "I think you'll see how your gift complements our rigorous academic experience and aligns perfectly with your value of sustainability."

You might never have tamed a school bully or managed a few million dollars' worth of women's accessories, but you have undoubtedly made a persuasive case for purchasing a piece of capital equipment, funding a new program, hiring a candidate above the minimum salary or giving a student who missed a payment deadline the chance to get back in the classroom to follow his or her dream. Each of these actions requires some measure of emotional and logical appeal in the evidence that you provided to make a persuasive case, but ultimately you got what you asked for, which leads me to the fifth and final tool in your possession.

You don't get if you don't ask

You can wear your institution proudly, tell richly descriptive stories that capture the rapt attention of an entire room and still walk away with nothing if you cannot make the ask. When I worked simultaneously in public radio and television, one of the most exciting experiences early on was my first pledge drive. Up to that point in my life, my family and I referred to these necessary interruptions to the regular flow of programming as "begging for dollars." Moving to the other side of the microphone and camera, as it were, was a bit like opening the curtain on the Wizard of Oz.

The on-air talent were provided mountains of data about the cost of programming, the limitations and restrictions of federal funding, the educational and entertainment impact on the lives of listeners and viewers, and precisely how much $1 or $100 a month would affect our stations' ability to continue to meet the expectations of our listening and viewing audiences. We memorized much of this, posted some of it on cue cards, and practiced off the air how we would toss our rhetoric from one speaker to another with a growing sense of urgency and need until finally someone would say just before the break concluded, "But we can't do it without you!" or "This is where you come in." Without the ask, we believed that the stations and our jobs could not survive. Without the ask, a donor would be left wondering, "Was this just a good story, or am I supposed to do something to ensure the next chapter gets written?"

Simply put, I learned that if I could look into a camera and ask a parent I did not even know and could not see to place a dollar value on the role that a purple dinosaur had played in improving his or her child's ability to get along with others and respect differences, then I could sit today in the presence of someone I know who has willingly invited me into his or her home or office and ask that individual to make an impact on economically disadvantaged students, with desperately needed instructional equipment, or upon generations of learners and teachers yet to come. Look into your well of experience, and you will likely find similar examples from which to draw. Think about something important that you asked for—a new bike when you were young, perhaps—and how good it felt when the answer was yes. Remember, too, that sometimes you'll hear "no," so expect defeats. Keep in mind, though, that "no" can mean "not yet," so remain persistent. The magical "yes" is worth it.

Finally, if you find that a few tools in your toolbox are rusty or just not as functional as you would like, plenty of help exists. You will and should turn often and openly to your development, advancement and marketing staff members for guidance, preparation and training. If you came into the presidency with a limited understanding of fundraising, there is no need to stumble through it alone. CASE and the American Association of Community Colleges are just two of the national organizations offering everything from multiday to one-hour institutes and courses to help CEOs be more proficient in securing public and private donations.

My own eclectic fundraising background has been strengthened by the mentors I have engaged primarily on development and alumni affairs issues. That these individuals all work a state or two away puts us in a comfortable, noncompetitive environment in which we can learn and lament together. Each of these mentoring relationships started with a phone call and an introduction—not unlike most of the relationship building I do as president.

Over time, you will come to realize that you always had it in you, and you may even be pretty good at fundraising. And if you should ever come to the point where you actually like doing it, be sure to pay it forward to at least one of the dozens of new colleagues each year who come into jobs like yours for the first time.

Chapter 10

HOW A MID-SIZE COLLEGE'S INVESTMENT IN ADVANCEMENT PAID OFF

By Catherine Chew

Navigating the first year as a new president is not unlike the experience of a first-year community college student. It can be tough. Assuming a first-time presidency in 2008, with frozen staff salaries, prohibited travel and limited expenditures for essential supplies and positions, was not an enviable position. The Great Recession and a fiscal landscape not witnessed since the Great Depression was the context for what would eventually become Craven Community College's successful advancement journey.

Leadership, strategic decision-making and assembling the right team were vital. As CEOs, we must have a vision, a deep commitment to students and staff, and an unwavering passion for the community college mission. We must also have the courage to make bold decisions and tough choices during difficult times.

Creating a vibrant institutional advancement office inclusive of the foundation, marketing, graphic design, grants and a Lifetime Learning Center has paid huge dividends. Our endowment has nearly doubled, and community support has never been stronger. Jim Collins says in his monograph *Good to Great and the Social Sectors*, "Greatness is not a function of circumstance. Greatness, it turns out, is largely a matter of conscious choice and discipline." Here is one mid-size community college's success story.

Our place within a community of contrasts

Craven Community College is located in eastern North Carolina and has two campuses: one in New Bern, a quaint retirement community with a population of approximately 30,000, and the other in Havelock, a military community that is home to Cherry Point Marine Corps Air Station and Fleet Readiness Center East, an aviation repair facility employing 3,500 civilians. The college serves more than 3,000 full-time equivalent students and 11,000 individuals through workforce development and customized training classes. The college's annual operating budget, most of which comes from the state, is $33 million. We are home to two "early colleges" along with North Carolina State University and East Carolina University programs, which offer baccalaureate degrees on site.

Despite being a small, rural county of only 100,000 people, Craven County has a diverse business and industry base that includes tourism, retail services, military, cultural arts and manufacturing. MOEN, Bosch-Siemens Home Appliances and Hatteras Yachts are located here.

The community, though, is one of many contrasts. There is a rich cultural legacy, with North Carolina's first capital and historical complex—Tryon Palace—along with deep southern traditions associated with the community's agrarian roots. Although outsiders have retired here, bringing vastly different personal and professional experiences and resources, a great deal of poverty and illiteracy are present as well.

Craven County can best be described as an emerging community, one that is stretching outside its comfort zone. It is filled with the most generous, philanthropic and giving people I have witnessed in a career that spans the Northeast, Midwest and South. It might also be described as a somewhat unworldly community, one that required a significant amount of education about both the expectations and the possibilities of what a college foundation might bring and accomplish at its community college.

A first-year president's initial thoughts

When I arrived at Craven, I immediately provided the board of trustees with five priorities, one of which was and has remained constant each year: increase the endowment. "If the endowment when I leave is the same as when I arrived, then you haven't been asking me the right questions," I told them. Advancement should be on every 21st-century community college leader's priority list. It is an essential role and perhaps the least understood in our sector—unlike in liberal arts or university institutions, which have a long history of fundraising and friend-raising.

In my initial days as president, I held group meetings with faculty and professional staff at both campuses to connect with people and to explain that I would embark on a "listening tour" with individuals. From my perspective, I wanted to emphasize three things, regardless of one's title or position: academic excellence, customer service and leadership.

I firmly believe that an institution's reputation for academic excellence far outweighs any marketing campaign. My philosophy is that students represent the heart of the institution, and the faculty represents the soul. Academic excellence would be our core.

Beyond the fundamental messages discussed early on, it was clear that a strategy would be needed to manage the huge budget deficits coming our way. Again, I suggested three areas of focus. First, we would hire a full-time grant writer (the college had never had one) to aggressively seek out federal grant opportunities. Second, we would need to have an entrepreneurial mindset and to think differently about our business. Third, we would need to grow our endowment and build sustainable resources that would see us through the difficult times and diminishing state resources.

Staying true to our core message and consistently repeating the mantra of academic excellence have fundamentally raised the college's profile within the community and people's belief in and commitment to us. Remaining steadfast on the strategic focus of growing the endowment while revitalizing the foundation board and creating a comprehensive institutional advancement office, we have enhanced our credibility and the college's importance to the community. We have made remarkable progress and experienced tremendous results, but we have surely not arrived. Craven Community College continues to be a joyful work in progress.

Our beginnings: Assess and invest

Within the first year of my presidency, I brought in an advancement consultant who spent two days conducting numerous internal and external interviews, and completing a comprehensive foundation audit. The investment in the study was money well spent, and the results and recommendations became our framework for moving forward.

Initially we had four full-time staff in what would be considered the advancement arm of the college: one executive director, one administrative assistant, a public information officer and a Lifetime Learning Center coordinator. After five years, despite consistent and significant budget deficits, we now have a full-fledged institutional advancement office with seven full-time staff and one part-time associate: one executive director, two administrative assistants, a director of marketing and development liaison, a graphic artist, a director of grants and strategic partnerships, and a director of the Lifetime Learning Center and cultural affairs.

If we were to benchmark our staffing levels with comparable community colleges, we'd likely be the envy of our peers. But community colleges continue to consistently underinvest in advancement efforts, including fundraising, marketing and communications, and alumni relations. My goal was to invest based on the potential of the college ... and of the community.

Adding to advancement meant taking away from other areas of the college, including faculty and administrative positions. However, it was a conscious and strategic decision. Experiencing $850,000 to $1 million budget cuts annually demanded that we leave positions vacant when someone resigned or retired. We also used more adjunct faculty and reallocated resources whenever possible. For example, we eliminated community enrichment courses and an associated full-time position. This move was especially controversial since we are located in a retirement community. The local paper ran numerous editorials on the subject, and I received many written complaints. We kept our focus by asking during budget deliberations what are "nice to do" versus "have to do" initiatives. We stayed the course despite the criticism and weathered the storm with a few battle scars to prove it.

Today our significant investment in advancement staff and resources is paying off in a big way. The endowment has grown, the internal campus campaign has increased each year and the external annual campaign continues to rise.

Although staff has been added since 2009, the lack of operational infrastructure was a huge void and has been built gradually over time. Like many community colleges, we were outdated and unsophisticated in our operations. Policies and systems were desperately needed and ranged from revising the foundation's bylaws to establishing accounting and tracking systems for donors, scholarships and funds. Members on the foundation board such as CPAs, certified financial planners and retired advancement professionals have volunteered and shared tremendous expertise, knowledge and time. We could not have accomplished what we have without their guidance and generosity. People's willingness to give and to be involved is always a source of inspiration. We have found that if you ask for assistance, most often, professionals are pleased to oblige.

Cultivating a strong and engaged foundation board was essential, but equally important was helping the board of trustees understand its role in fundraising and friend-raising. There was resistance in the early days of this discussion. We began this process slowly by creating an annual social event and dinner attended by the college's Executive Leadership Team, trustees and foundation board members along with their spouses at the president's home. Now, either a trustee or foundation board member hosts the social. Next, we incorporated professional development training, bringing in outside university advancement expertise during the trustees' annual retreat. The trustee chair's role and support have been critically important in this process. Today, after six years, we can finally say that 100 percent of our board of trustees contribute to the college foundation. Changing a mindset takes time.

Our successes: A few best practices

Being a female executive leader comes with some unique challenges. That is why former Hewlett-Packard CEO Carly Fiorina's book, *Tough Choices*, resonated with me as the institutional transformation began. She wrote, "All triumphs are made of the same stuff: the right support, the right team, the determination to achieve the goal, lots of really hard work. And all triumphs are much more about choice than they are about chance." We had all the ingredients that Fiorina describes as we created two very successful initiatives at Craven Community College.

The Community Fabric Awards event and the VIP Ambassador Program were proposed to the foundation (after experiencing similar, yet different models at other institutions) and adapted to our community. Not only have they brought additional resources, but they have brought the college lasting friendships and recognition. They could be easily adapted to another community.

Community Fabric Awards

Our most recent Community Fabric Awards event attracted more than 600 people for a luncheon to recognize a business leader, a civic leader and an education leader. An anonymous selection committee chooses the recipients, and I have the honor of calling to tell them about their award. Their reactions are always the same: expressions of humility and honor.

The event has become a popular community celebration—with vast media coverage—that showcases the essence of what makes Craven County special. We always feature two students who share their community college story, student ambassadors who escort guests to their tables, and a wonderful performance by our singing ambassador group. This "warm fuzzy" day is comparable to graduation day and is a win-win for the college and the community. Through sponsorships and individual tickets, the college netted more than $40,000 at the latest event.

More important than the resources garnered, we introduce newcomers to the community college mission and we have an opportunity to highlight on center stage the college's first-class quality.

The Community Fabric Awards event has become the college's signature event for fundraising and friend-raising. A golf tournament might be a more traditional (and more common) fundraiser, but it reaches a very specialized segment. The beauty of the Community Fabric Awards is that it occurs during most people's lunch breaks, so they return to their regular workday having had a "feel-good" lunch. They leave impressed by the college and inspired by the students and the honorees.

VIP Ambassador Program

Our VIP Ambassador Program was launched in 2012 and is organized by the institutional advancement office. It is co-facilitated by the executive director of advancement and a long-tenured department chair. The program has been extremely well received, and now community members call us, asking if they can be invited to participate—exactly the position we want to be in. The program is by "special invitation of the president" and allows for 15 participants. The executive director of advancement and I choose individuals whom we believe would be terrific ambassadors and spokespersons for the college in the community.

No financial commitment is expected, and participants' only requirement is to attend (and participate in) four half-day sessions during a four-month timeframe. During the program, participants are introduced to both campuses through tours, program overviews and student presentations. At the conclusion of the program, our

VIP Ambassadors graduate with a certificate during a final celebratory luncheon with fellow VIP alumni.

As a direct result of one ambassador referral, the college has secured the largest legacy gift in its history. During their lifetime, the donors are financially supporting three student ambassadors each year and are leaving a $1.2 million bequest to the college in their estate. A second VIP referral has resulted in the addition of an extremely qualified and philanthropic individual as a member of the foundation board. Another substantial legacy gift is currently under way with this new foundation board member. You might say the VIP program has been a great connector.

The Community Fabric Awards event and the VIP Ambassador Program have been great additions to the college's outreach efforts. We are making friends daily and spreading the word about the mission of community colleges and the exceptional things being done for students, businesses and communities by Craven Community College.

Lessons learned: It's about people and relationships

Presidents, by the nature of their position, must be change agents of sorts. We also can be impatient human beings. Perhaps we are just wired that way. The challenge remains the same: When bringing about change in any organization, how do you manage the timing and the pace? How do you find the right balance? At the seasoned age of 62 years, I would suggest that it all depends on the unique circumstances one inherits, but I also suggest being bold.

It is a pretty sure bet that any change initiative will take longer than one expects. It's like a home improvement project. It always takes twice as long as you think.

Despite our successes, Craven Community College's advancement journey has not been a bed of roses every step of the way. As with many situations, it often comes down to people. As Jim Collins would say, do you have the right people in the right seats on the bus? Finding experienced, top-notch advancement professionals is not easy and they do not come cheaply.

One of the challenges of not living in a metropolitan area is recruiting the most qualified or experienced individuals. It took us a couple of tries to find the appropriate advancement professional to lead our team, and this made for a bumpy road for a few years. Do not settle for someone who doesn't have the appropriate skill set that will ensure your success, because asking for money is not just anyone's forte; it requires a special person.

Believing in the mission of community colleges and having a passion for students are necessary and foundational qualities. So, too, is the ability to relate to and interact with a variety of people, including political leaders, business CEOs, civic leaders, wealthy individuals and those with limited means.

If you cannot find a leader with advancement experience, growing someone who has the potential is a viable alternative. Donor development and advancement initiatives are a long-term commitment and investment. Working with organizations, such as the Council for Advancement and Support of Education (CASE), drawing on professionals in the field who can serve as mentors and benchmarking other institutions with mature advancement programs are ways in which a new president can build and cultivate a sustainable advancement operation. These strategies are a way to develop a new advancement professional and they are a way for a new president, without advancement experience, to learn. It is good to be patient and to recognize that it will take time and sustained effort.

Whether you are establishing an annual or a capital campaign, creating a planned giving program, growing scholarships or cultivating donors, ultimately, it is ALL about relationships.

Thinking back on my early career when I was active in a local arts council, I was asked to sell raffle tickets for a fundraising event that required making cold calls. I was terrible at it, despite the coaching assistance from my partner at the time, who was an astute broker. We both ended up buying my tickets instead of selling them to others.

As a president, I've come a long way. It is not difficult for me to "sell" Craven Community College and to ask others in the community to help us. Why? Because we have a great institution and we are providing a great service to students, businesses, the military and our community at large. We need them, and they need us. It is a mutually beneficial relationship: We strengthen each other and we enrich the community together. It really is not difficult to ask, if one genuinely believes in and has a passion for what one is selling. The Congleton Courtyard sculpture garden and the Margaret Stancil Rose Garden at Craven are fine examples of successful relationship-building.

Final thoughts

With deep sincerity and great honesty, I can say that one of the most gratifying experiences of the presidency has been working with the foundation board members and engaging with the college's institutional advancement efforts. The opportunity to meet new people, to cultivate potential donors and to witness firsthand the philanthropy of individuals is inspirational beyond words.

The people I have come to know and the relationships that have been created are heartfelt and lasting. The gifts and generosity of our donors are a reminder of what is, very simply, good in the world. In a world that often feels out of control, these donors represent a life worth living.

Perhaps you feel as I do: Working as a servant leader in a community college setting is a calling and an honor. In their book *Encouraging the Heart*, James M. Kouzes and Barry Z. Posner write, "Leadership is not about a position or a place. It's an attitude and a sense of responsibility for making a difference."

As we lead our 21st-century institutions and work hard every day to make a difference, developing an institutional advancement office and growing the endowment are not options. State resources are diminishing, and demands for greater accountability through performance-based funding are here to stay. It is imperative and wise to establish a thriving advancement operation within our colleges; in fact, it would be imprudent to do otherwise.

Chapter 11

ESTABLISHING A CLIMATE FOR PUBLIC-PRIVATE PARTNERSHIPS

By Bryan D. Albrecht

Often referred to as "the machine shop of the world," southeastern Wisconsin has a rich history in the development of the world's manufacturing industry, making the region where Gateway Technical College was founded a hotbed of industrial development across many industry sectors.

The Nash Rambler was produced in southeastern Wisconsin, home of American Motors, Chrysler and Golden Books. Racine is widely known for J.I. Case tractors, Modine heat transfer systems and InSinkErator waste disposal systems.

To support the need for a highly skilled workforce, Gateway Technical College—like most community colleges—maintains a comprehensive approach to education and training. Unlike many community colleges, though, Gateway long ago embraced the notion of public-private partnerships. It's part of our DNA, and something I have continued enthusiastically since becoming president in 2006.

Partnerships with such companies as J.I. Case, Modine, Snap-on, SC Johnson, Ocean Spray, InSinkErator, Trane, Twin Disc and Pioneer Products have lasted for decades, and they serve as a foundation for new partnerships with the likes of Uline, Kenall, Amazon and UNFI.

Whereas some community colleges today seek public-private partnerships to offset declining revenues in other areas, I see these as relationships vital to the success of the college and the community, and a natural extension of the community college mission.

I'll describe a few of the unique partnerships in this chapter, but it is important to recognize that Gateway has replicated the basic elements of the model with several global companies in an effort to build a talent pipeline for local industries.

Gateway Technical College serves 24,000 students annually in over 60 degree areas in the tri-county region of southeastern Wisconsin, including Racine, Kenosha and Walworth counties. Founded in 1911, Gateway celebrates a century-old mission of collaboration to ensure economic growth and viability by providing education, training, leadership and technological resources to meet the changing needs of students, employers and communities.

I believed that the focus on workforce development and partnerships was important to the college's advancement and growth, so during a board retreat in my first year as president we revised the following Ends Statement to better reflect our new vision: "Gateway will provide leadership in tri-county community and workforce development through partnerships with business, industry, labor, and community organizations to support economic development."

Since I became president, Gateway has elevated the ideals of business partnerships into strategic business alliances that benefit our corporate partners, our college and our community. Any community college can—and should—be continually building similar alliances, regardless of whether it has major manufacturers or global headquarters in its service area.

The four cornerstones

My philosophy rests on four cornerstones that have sustained and in many ways built a national network of community college public-private partnerships. The four elements are not surprising, but the approach to sharing our values surrounding each element differentiates us from other more traditional partnerships like advisory committees, philanthropic donations or selling naming rights for a building project.

The cornerstone elements are belief, trust, transparency and sustainability. These four simple words can be used to describe any successful relationship, but the key here is *relationship.* Successful public-private partnerships must be developed as a relationship if they are to maintain meaning and grow over time. Recognizing that companies change just as college priorities change is essential to the evolution of that relationship.

Belief

Believe in your mission, vision and instincts regarding where your greatest opportunities exist. Your window of opportunity is short, so act quickly but strategically. Successful relationships will present additional opportunities, because people and companies want to be associated with successful organizations.

In 2014 Kenall Manufacturing held a groundbreaking ceremony a few miles from our college to announce a new facility employing more than 600 people. During the event, Kenall CEO Jim Hawkins specifically mentioned us as important to his plans. "We are excited to move as soon as possible so that we can begin adding new jobs to Kenosha and the surrounding area, including recruitment from neighboring Gateway Technical College." This is not the only time a corporate partner has identified Gateway as a strategic component of their growth. Also in 2014, Liz Uihlein, president of Uline Inc., said in announcing a million-square-foot expansion, "We recognize the state and county for establishing schools like Gateway and Carthage for educating the talent to fill the jobs of today." Public statements like these serve as a testament that our partnerships are respected and valued.

Believe in your administration, faculty and staff. Developing the trust needed to implement and sustain new relationships can take many people at multiple levels in an organization. Without full transparency, it can be difficult for everyone to understand and appreciate what the relationship may mean to the college, a specific program and the students receiving the education and training. Everyone involved in the partnership must believe in the shared purpose and vision for success. I intentionally share the leadership and responsibility of sustaining these relationships with others at the college. It helps to secure ownership and educate team members about issues that may not be easily visible from outside the circle. The more people who believe in your vision, the easier your job will be to lead the organization.

Trust

Trust is the key to everything in a relationship. Unfortunately, public-private partnerships are inherently surrounded by mistrust. You will hear excuses like, "We tried that before" or "Corporations are not willing to invest in publicly funded organizations" or "Companies are not willing to share their intellectual property." Trust must be demonstrated at the top. As the CEO of your college, it is essential that you establish relationships with the CEOs in your community. Their trust is essential to your success. A critical turning point in my career was when I decided to terminate a partnership because trust was not established. The branding that came with the association of a global partner was not as important as the trust we needed to sustain the partnership. Having the courage to recognize that will send a powerful message about your leadership integrity throughout your college and community. Corporate partners place a high value on brand integrity. If they lend you their brand, they trust your integrity.

I also have built trust and credibility by serving on more than 50 local, state and national boards—many of which are industry related. Each experience adds to my network of professional contacts and potential partnerships. Managing the time it takes to be effective to the organizations I serve, as well as building a stronger base for Gateway, is an integrated process. It is not one or the other, but a value-added process for both. Every board and committee I serve on is a potential growth opportunity for our college.

Transparency

Transparency is defined as *readily understood.* Relationships can be complicated and require extra care in effectively communicating the goals, processes and outcomes desired. The partners should identify measurable sustaining factors. Some examples might include whether the relationship is included in business unit goals; whether the partnership is clearly communicated throughout both organizations; whether benchmarks or measures are in place; whether the investment strategy is diversified to include business development, philanthropy, research and development; whether student outcomes have improved; and whether the relationship adds brand value for both organizations. Provide your corporate partners with progress reports that specifically address the goals and growth strategies of the relationship. Without data it is difficult to quantify the value of the relationship. Remember, there needs to be value for all partners.

Sustainability

To be effective and sustainable, public-private partnerships should be formalized in writing. Formal agreements clarify goals and provide a framework of expectations. The agreement should provide meaningful action plans and guiding principles for managing the relationship, as well as for growing (and ending) it. Beyond the formal agreement, collaborative partnerships should link to existing initiatives that promote the broader workforce and economic development agendas of each organization. Connecting to organizational strategies and performance goals will help to ensure that the partnership programs and activities are viewed as part of the organization's measures of success. Keep in mind that every partnership should be of equal advantage to all participants. Too often education seeks a one-sided relationship and does not consider the strategic, long-term advantages to each partner, nor does education typically recognize the increased return on investment for all concerned.

Sustaining a public-private relationship is the ultimate measure of success. Will your relationship survive through leadership changes, economic changes or corporate restructuring? My relationship with Snap-on, for example, transitioned between two CEOs due to clear and purposeful communications.

Building on the cornerstones

Belief, trust, transparency and sustainability—these four words collectively define the public-private partnerships established at Gateway Technical College. As a college president, you are charged with fostering growth for your college while meeting the diverse needs of the communities you serve. I can't begin to describe what success might look like elsewhere, but I hope to inspire you to look beyond traditional models of business partnerships.

To give you a sense of how our model works, the next four sections describe successful relationships we have developed.

Snap-on

Snap-on, a company founded in Kenosha, Wisconsin, in 1910 to support the emerging auto industry, has partnered with Gateway since the 1960s, but it wasn't until 2006 that the partnership evolved into a strategic relationship. The watershed moment occurred when then–Snap-on CEO Jack Michaels visited Gateway, and I shared my vision for developing a public-private partnership that would transform training for automotive technicians. The goal was to spark curiosity backed by a model that embraced a business need of Snap-on's with a training gap that we had within Gateway.

Snap-on had introduced a new tool in the diagnostic assessment of automobile systems, but their technical training capacity was not meeting their needs. Gateway was in a pivotal position as well. We could invest in a new auto technician program or close a core program that had operated for more than 60 years but had not kept up with appropriate facilities, current equipment or industry employment needs. Snap-on's CEO and I both believed that we had a need to leverage each other's strengths.

That shared belief remains intact under the current leadership of CEO Nick Pinchuk. Pinchuk has embraced and challenged us to build a system that would have a national reach. Within months the National Coalition of Certification Centers (NC3) was formed, and Gateway began training and certifying community and technical college instructors from throughout the nation in Snap-on diagnostics.

Belief and trust built on a common understanding and clear expectations serves as the foundation for sustaining the relationship. To date, more than 900 instructors have been Snap-on certified, more than 14,000 student technicians have been certified and more than 200 colleges are delivering one or more of the 19 Snap-on certifications developed through NC3. Gateway in partnership with Snap-on invested in a new facility with a name that reminds us of our work still to be completed: the Horizon Center, which represents the transformation of Gateway's automotive and aviation programs. The horizon, where the land (auto) and sky (aviation) meet, is forever changing, a reminder that helps keep professional development at the center of our NC3 mission. This investment continues today through a signed agreement between Gateway and Snap-on to support the center as well as NC3 program development.

Trane

Seeing the success of the relationship between Snap-on and Gateway, Trane, a world leader in air conditioning systems and services, approached us to see if we could meet a need in their industry. The HVAC industry is expected to need up to 50,000 technicians in the next 10 years to meet industry demands and Baby Boomer retirements.

With over 100 years of experience, Trane has many core strengths, including training, but they lacked the ability to increase capacity at a rate that would allow them to fill the skills gap. Gateway and NC3 began to develop a curriculum in an emerging field for Trane called building automation, and we now offer two certifications. Gateway also now hosts the NC3 Train the Trainer conference each summer to give instructors from throughout the United States the experience of a world-class facility and curriculum. More important, it affords instructors the opportunity to network with industry leaders like Trane and Snap-on. Trane has since expanded the model to include 12 training centers at community colleges also delivering building automation certifications.

InSinkErator

With more than 200 training partnerships, not all of our partnerships are built on a single model of industry certifications, but they are all built on the same four elements. Founded in Racine, Wisconsin, and now a global company, InSinkErator has worked with Gateway for more than 20 years. At their Racine manufacturing facility, employees at all levels are in need of refreshed math skills. In response to this need, InSinkErator established an onsite classroom and contracted with Gateway to provide courses specific to math and other related technical competencies. Courses are determined from employee assessments, corporate growth strategies and new technology investments.

The trust in Gateway allows for open dialogue about meeting InSinkErator's other training needs. Gateway instructors have embraced the culture and values of InSinkErator, customizing the experience as a corporate investment in the company's workforce.

SC Johnson

Also founded in Racine, SC Johnson has been manufacturing household cleaning products for more than 120 years. The relationship with Gateway started with the development of a corporate college that led to a Bellwether Award by the League for Innovation. The latest milestone: a $1.7 million corporate gift from SC Johnson to support a community training initiative called Boot Camps.

Boot Camps were developed in partnership with local industries to address the unemployment and underemployment conditions of the inner city of Racine. SC Johnson CEO Fisk Johnson recognized that Gateway's commitment to building a local workforce is important for Racine as well as for SC Johnson. For a company like SC Johnson to have the belief, trust and confidence in us to address the community's important social needs sends a powerful message to our employees. Gateway's ability to transform a community along with our largest corporate citizen has positioned our college to reap benefits for years.

Where to begin

Getting started can often be the most intimidating. Organizations such as the Council for Advancement and Support of Education (CASE) offer workshops and seminars on how to develop fundraising strategies, set goals and secure donations. Any president or foundation director should seek professional development to gain a perspective on the various types of fundraising strategies and to learn some of the successful techniques shared by others. Fundraising is not necessarily the same as establishing long-term public-private partnerships, but trustees and the community will look for how much money is brought to the college through these efforts. Capital campaigns, philanthropic donations and naming rights for facilities are all great ways to generate resources for your college, but that does not mean they will lead to the development of a long-term public-private partnership.

These relationships and partnerships take time to develop, and they require a plan for successful implementation. Keep in mind what I call the ABCs for successful partnerships:

- Assess your opportunities.
- Be clear about your vision.
- Create a value (return on investment) for every "ask."

The first step is to assess what opportunities are available to you. Do you have specific program needs that align with local companies? Are there personal relationships you or others in your college have with corporate executives? Is there a change taking place within your local community that can serve as a draw to your college? Understanding your needs is critical to the next step.

The second step is to be clear about your vision for the partnership. I cannot stress enough the importance of being clear on why the relationship is important to the greater vision for the college, company and community. Document this step in writing. It does not have to be a formal white paper, but you will need to put your ideas and vision on paper so that they can be shared within both organizations. Clarity begins with the first conversation and is a requirement for the next step.

The third step is to create and express the value of the partnership. It may be easy for you to see the value because the partnership benefits your college directly. Your success will be measured by your ability to express value to your corporate partner. This is the business case for your vision. Remember that a public-private partnership is more than a philanthropic donation to your college. The goal is to align the business outcomes for both organizations. Your partnerships will be sustainable if you can articulate strategic business reasons and demonstrate the return on investment for all parties. Beyond that, you also should provide opportunity for organizational growth.

Each relationship is unique and takes individual nurturing. At Gateway we have established a team approach to nurturing each relationship. Together we have identified several value touch points for our corporate partners and take pride in reporting our success to them on a regular basis. Growing our relationships requires increasing the value of the touch points. As president of Gateway, I am always looking for the opportunity to tell our story, and the success stories here are seemingly endless. The community and technical college environment provides a compelling case for more public-private partnerships. Community and technical colleges play a big role in filling the talent pipeline; some might say we are a supply-chain necessity. I have had success sharing the value of Gateway with industry partnerships by being honest and clear about our vision for meeting the workforce needs of the communities we serve. I stress that I want our college to be a solution for the needs of business and industry, and that we all have an investment in securing our community's future workforce.

Transforming an industry starts with believing that there is a need so compelling that your survival depends on finding a solution. Successful public-private relationships are grounded in trust and a shared vision. Trane saw in Gateway what successful relationships looked like through Snap-on and built on that commitment to establish a program that met their specific needs. To have a company like Trane replicate the model established with Snap-on confirmed my belief that the four cornerstones of belief, trust, transparency and sustainability allow for relationships to take new shapes and build off each other. Transforming a community or technical college is no easy task. Leveraging your success to spur additional growth is critical. As a college president, you don't have enough time or energy to create new models for every partnership. Establish your cornerstones and link the common values of each of your community partners to build a vibrant network of community and industry support.

Chapter 12

TRANSFORMING A "NO" INTO A "YES"

The Presidential Pursuit of Fundraising Excellence

By Robert H. Sandel

The process of transforming a donor's initial "no" into a transformational "yes" encompassed more than a decade of leadership, institutional change and cultivation. The art of philanthropy has proven to be a combination of knowledge, time and interpersonal skills that equate to being the gift within a gift. Experiences proved, time and time again, that fundraising is an art as opposed to a science. Fundraising strategies can be taught; however, a scientific formula that leads to the successful solicitation of a gift does not exist. Intuitively knowing when to solicit a gift extends from the insight gained throughout the development of a relationship with a potential donor.

I have yet to meet anyone who planned to pursue fundraising as a profession, but I have met many who became fundraisers due to being in a leadership role. In 1992 I became the president of Mountain Empire Community College in Virginia, after serving the South Carolina Technical College System as vice president of workforce development and vice president of academic and student affairs. As president, I was thrust into the role of rookie fundraiser and chief fundraising officer.

Lessons learned at Mountain Empire proved instrumental to my later success securing a $5 million gift at another institution.

Mountain Empire, a rural college in Big Stone Gap, is considered by many Virginians to be located in the *old southwest* of the Commonwealth. It is closer in highway mileage to the state capitals of seven other states than to Virginia's capitol in Richmond. Big Stone Gap encompassed 5,548 residents in 2013 and maintained a median family income of $27,060. The largest industry is coal mining. Mountain Empire serves four counties and three cities, yet it remains the focal point for the residents. The enrollment of Mountain Empire, when I assumed the presidency, was approximately 1,800 full-time equivalent (FTE) students and a headcount of approximately 3,000.

When I began at Mountain Empire, I recall overlooking the campus and contemplating how to most effectively position the college to move the region—our service district—forward. I concluded that the development of trustworthy relationships with faculty, staff and key members of the local community would position the institution in a more prominent role as an economic driver.

Mountain Empire's foundation began soaring upon hiring an executive director whose background in resource development and political affairs further engaged the board of directors in the identification and solicitation of major donors. The executive director's primary responsibilities were to supplement the scope of the college's budget through funds raised and the receipt of local, state and federal grants. It was the first time that the value of resource development was emphasized.

In collaboration with the foundation board of directors and the executive director, I initiated the college's first major gifts campaign. I solicited the lead gift for the campaign from a private foundation dedicated to supporting Wise and Lee counties. That foundation maintained assets of approximately $25 million at the time, yet it was known for awarding few major gifts and numerous smaller gifts. The college, prior to the campaign, received an initial unrestricted gift of $40,000 from that foundation to fund the purchase of a Steinway piano for college use at special functions. This $40,000 donation occurred after my wife, Jane, and I hosted select board members of the foundation at our home and featured a Steinway pianist who played our baby grand piano beautifully. The prospective donors were overwhelmed by the talent of the masterful pianist but more so by the thoughtfulness of organizing such a production in their honor.

I use that example to underscore my belief in building solid relationships. Years later, I solicited a $1 million donation from the board of the private foundation and received the following response: "We wondered when someone would ask for a million-dollar donation. ..." The campaign was launched immediately following the solicitation with a public acknowledgment of the gift. The positive outcome of this philanthropic process did not result from following a scientific or mathematic formula. The process was artful; the *gift within the gift* was the development of a meaningful relationship.

Among the lessons learned at Mountain Empire: Think big.

The Mountain Empire foundation currently ranks third in terms of assets, compared to the other 23 institutions comprising the Virginia Community College System. During my tenure the executive director was promoted to vice president of institutional advancement, the number of foundation staff members more than doubled and salaries were funded by an unrestricted asset base of which I solicited approximately $3 million. The team of employees and community members dedicated to Mountain Empire Community College raised the profile of and made the case for the college's need for additional resources. I am proud to observe the progress of the college and believe my contributions through philanthropy further positioned the college for excellence.

I left Mountain Empire in 2001, no longer a rookie fundraiser, to become president of Virginia Western Community College. My nine years of service as president and chief fundraising officer at Mountain Empire taught me how to ask for large amounts of money without flinching, as well as how raising a college's local profile is predicated on the development of successful relationships.

A 10-year challenge begins

I began at Virginia Western Community College on July 1, 2001, examining the campus structure and initiating relationships with local board members, faculty and staff. I felt the potential growth of the college was limitless and remember thinking, "I've stepped into a gold mine." I always believed that success resulted from mining an entire mountain, not by finding one golden nugget and trying to live off of it for a lifetime. I was given gold in Virginia Western and was determined to increase the awareness of the college's value. My goal was to motivate internal and external stakeholders to make a solid investment in the lives of students.

It was a process that took more than a decade.

Virginia Western's 70-acre main campus is located in the urban city of Roanoke, with campus sites in the rural areas of Botetourt and Franklin counties. Roanoke is the largest municipality in southwestern Virginia and is the principal municipality of the Roanoke Metropolitan Statistical Area. The college's service district includes the cities of Roanoke and Salem, and the counties of Botetourt, Craig, Franklin and Roanoke. Roanoke is considered the commercial and cultural hub of the majority of southwestern Virginia and portions of southern West Virginia. Roanoke City, for example, in 2013, maintained a population of 98,465 and a median household income of $38,265.

The enrollment of Virginia Western when I assumed the presidency was approximately 3,200 FTE students and a head count of approximately 10,000. The college in 2013–2014 maintained an FTE of 5,050 and a head count of approximately 13,000. Roanoke is the primary provider of business and health care services and retail trade for southwestern Virginia. Virginia Western currently leads Virginia's 23 community colleges in enrollment growth and maintains the second largest enrollment of the higher education institutions in western Virginia, the first of which is Virginia Polytechnic Institute and State University (Virginia Tech). Eighty-five percent of Virginia Western's graduates serve as members of the regional workforce.

A colleague of mine, a former college leader, advised me to keep the traditional community college image, which implied that we should take a secondary role in prominence and leadership capacities in the community compared to four-year colleges and universities. In other words, the public and private university sector presidents were those who should engage in chief executive officer roundtables, as members in leadership positions on prominent boards such as the Roanoke Chamber of Commerce and as members of social clubs.

I, on the other hand, was dedicated to eliminating the long-standing stigma of a community college education not being as noteworthy as the quality education offered by four-year institutions. My involvement in leadership roles in various community organizations has given the college additional credibility. Networking with members in these organizations has been instrumental in repositioning the college's image. As a result, today we have a foundation board that is envied by other organizations.

Overlooking the city of Roanoke by 1,045 feet is the world's largest freestanding illuminated star, the Roanoke or Mill Mountain Star. Roanoke was named the "Star City of the South" after the construction of the star. I was hired to reenergize the college as a waning star. I began by cultivating relationships with members of the Virginia Western's foundation and governing boards.

Members of the foundation board introduced me to key business leaders and local businesses. The total assets of the Virginia Western Educational Foundation in 2001 were approximately $1 million, and a major campaign had never been pursued. I worked diligently to initiate the college's first major gift campaign, which was launched in 2003.

The chair of the major gifts campaign was the chief executive officer of a local gas company and an alumnus of Virginia Western who went on to earn a master's degree at Virginia Commonwealth University. The campaign chair's credentials and professional journey are impressive; however, his professionalism, integrity and kind nature are most admirable. Hence, I was fortunate to be paired with such a stellar community business leader who agreed to share my professional mission: to raise the profile of Virginia Western within the local community.

The campaign chair scheduled a meeting with what we thought was a top prospect: the head of a regional medical facilities company who also served as a co-trustee for a family trust that awarded funds for the purpose of enhancing local economic development. The prospect was an advocate of higher education and served on the board of visitors of the University of Virginia and Virginia Tech. He also served in the leading role for the Virginia Business Higher Education Council during which "Grow by Degrees" was launched, with the principal goal of awarding an additional 100,000 degrees by 2025 in Virginia. The prospect also served as a member of the State Council of Higher Education for Virginia and as a member of the Gubernatorial Commission on Higher Education Reform, Innovation and Investment.

I looked forward to meeting this person for the first time, as I knew of his numerous accomplishments and contributions to higher education and Roanoke. I relied on the campaign chair, who served on numerous local boards with the prospect, to solicit the gift in support of the college's newly announced major gifts campaign. After introductions and casual conversation, I provided an overview of the college's successes and emphasized the primary goal of the first campaign—to increase student access to Virginia Western through the provision of scholarships.

Then came the unexpected.

The prospect then shared his perspective about our funding. Since Virginia Western received approximately 80 percent of funding from the state and 20 percent from tuition and fees, he posited that community colleges, including Virginia Western, did not need additional funding. The meeting ended quickly, and the campaign chair and I were on our way.

We were clearly disappointed in the rejection by one of the most influential business leaders in Roanoke. The meeting confirmed that I had my work cut out for me, so I began preparing the college to serve as the primary education economic engine for the Roanoke region. *I was on a mission.*

First, look inward

The relationships developed with faculty and staff engendered high-performing teamwork, which led the college to share an institutional vision, mission and core values. The college-wide strategic planning process was transparent for the first time since the college's inception in 1966. The process was supported by national, local and institutional data and a broad-based representation of students, faculty, staff, and local community members and business leaders. My most important job was to lead the process of executing the strategic plan by being deeply engaged in the internal and external operations of the college and having robust discussions with employees, which led to an intellectually honest and realistic working environment.

I learned early in my career that hiring the most qualified employees was key to an institution's success and is a responsibility that should not be delegated. The college's enrollment began to increase, new partnerships were developed with the local community and facilities were renovated. I created an executive director position for the Virginia Western Educational Foundation and hired someone who had a strong knowledge base in fundraising, maintained strong board relations skills and developed, with the board and me, what is now a nationally recognized scholarship program—the Community College Access Program (CCAP). I approved the hiring of a bookkeeper and three coordinators (of development, alumni and development, and scholarships and CCAP). A major gifts campaign to support CCAP was launched in 2008.

I received approval from the state for the construction of a $28 million facility to house the health and science programs. The college's academic affairs unit began eliminating programs that were not in high demand and creating new programs to serve as a feeder to the Roanoke region's primary employment market—health care. I also strengthened the full-time base of the faculty and provided faculty and staff with additional support such as financial resources for professional development. A grants development office was created, offering faculty and staff the opportunity to receive support in the pursuit of grants. Virginia Western was awarded grants from the National Science Foundation, the U.S. Department of Labor, the U.S. Department of Education and the National Endowment for the Arts. Faculty grants, over the course of 10 years, exceeded $15 million.

I hired a vice president of institutional advancement to further integrate the following functions: fundraising, grants, marketing, public information, graphic design, events and strategic planning. I sought a qualified resource development and marketing professional with a strong understanding of the community college and its mission.

The vice president, board members, and I led CCAP to serve the college's entire service district for the first time since its inception. The public-private partnership of CCAP received national recognition in 2014 for its impact on the workforce and economic development. The vice president, board members and I also focused on strengthening the foundation's endowment. We knew that Virginia Western's future of accessibility and affordability was in our hands.

Throughout the decade, I encountered the previously mentioned major gift prospect (the one who said "no") during several local CEO meetings, community functions and meetings regarding the economic development of the region. He saw that my focus remained on raising the profile of Virginia Western, providing skilled graduates, and strengthening workforce development offerings to business and industry. The previous campaign chair, who served as foundation board member emeritus at the time, suggested that we meet again with the prospect—this time to discuss a possible $5 million donation, but also to invite him and his son, who was a co-trustee of the family trust, to the college to visit. The meeting was successful in that the prospect seemed interested and was open to the visit.

Our second chance

The vice president, board members and I prepared diligently for the visit. We did our homework! We presented the prospect and his son the request for funding for scholarships aligned with the focal point of the family trust. The prospect's brother, prior to his death, dedicated the trust to enhancing the economic development of the Roanoke Valley. Hence, the vice president, board members and I described the potential impact of the $5 million donation by explaining the growth of Virginia Western over the course of a decade and presenting data highlighting Virginia Western as second to Virginia Tech as the institution of choice within the Roanoke-Blacksburg region.

The $5 million gift, we explained, would

- help offset a decline in state funding, which had dropped to 40 percent of our budget;
- nearly double the foundation's assets;
- double the number of scholarships offered to students; and
- single-handedly move the foundation from 16th to fourth in the ranking of educational foundations among the 24 in the Virginia Community College System.

It was 10 years in the making, but we got our "yes." And it was worth the wait.

In 2012 the trust committed $5 million over five years to Virginia Western to establish scholarships in the areas of science, technology, math and health care (STEM-H). The gift is the largest donation dedicated to scholarships in the history of the Virginia Community College System and one of the largest for community college scholarships in the country. I consider this to be the community college gift of a lifetime and potentially the community college gift of *my* lifetime.

The donor was quoted in the local newspaper asserting, "Like all communities, the economic future of the Roanoke Valley is dependent on the steps taken to ensure success. The economy is a knowledge-based economy, and therefore, a focus on a more skilled and educated workforce is a must."

If I had given up after the first "no," as might be expected, then the gift would never have occurred. Lesson learned: Sometimes "no" actually means "not yet."

The new facility for science and health professions was dedicated to the donor's family. The dedication ceremony included colleagues of the donor and his family, who spoke in honor of his numerous contributions to Virginia's higher education system.

I will never forget the donor's address at the ceremony. He said that students should be provided with the opportunity to complete higher education without the burden of debt—and that required private investments. He also said,

> "Please don't leave with the impression that $5 million is sufficient. It is not. Bobby Sandel, his staff and faculty do a great job. We have a well performing community college in place and this building will enhance the students' education. However, the buildings don't provide scholarships and that's the college's pressing need. We must triple the trust gift and do it soon. Scholarships lead to an educated workforce and an educated workforce leads to economic development. That's an example of what I mean when I say we determine our own destiny when it comes to enhancing our economy and our standard of living.
>
> "... The current focus on workforce development is critical to economic development and Virginia Western is critical to economic development and Virginia Western can and should lead this economic development effort in our region. We can do this, and I ask each of you to step forward and help make Virginia Western the best community college in Virginia. It needs your service and your contribution. If we do our part, the college will return a vibrant economy to our region."

The $5 million gift and the dedication ceremony represent a pivotal point in the history of Virginia Western. Virginia Western was recognized as a major provider of education access, quality and opportunity and as a viable economic player in the Roanoke Valley. The pride in the college's success pervaded the entire organization and provided momentum to our college and fundraising efforts that continues today. I maintain the deepest gratitude to the donor and family for believing in Virginia Western, but more so for their dedication to the enhancement of students' lives.

The role of the community college president in fundraising will only become more vital to the institution's success in the years ahead. I urge presidents to actively engage with key business leaders to further connect colleges with business and industry. Of course, hiring the right people for the right jobs is also critical. Human capital has the potential to yield the strongest return on investment.

The art of philanthropy extends from the development of relationships, the personalization of the solicitation and an intuitive sense about the donor's commitment. Effective timing is key to the success of fundraising efforts: The ask should not occur too soon and, therefore, should not be rushed. Shakespeare's Jaques, in *As You Like It*, claimed: "All the world's a stage, And all the men and women merely players: They have their exits and their entrances; And one man in his time plays many parts."

The 21st century continues to shed light on the need for and importance of community colleges as leaders of high-demand career and technical programming. Colleagues, take the present time, pull out your canvases and paintbrushes, and enjoy the art of philanthropy. The time is now for you to paint the future of community college education on the world's stage.

Chapter 13

THE CAPITAL CAMPAIGN THAT SHOULD NOT HAVE SUCCEEDED

By Carol A. Churchill

The poet Elizabeth Barrett Browning counted the ways of love. *Late Show* host David Letterman made the Top Ten list famous. But so far, no one has tallied up the ways in which a capital campaign could fail ... until Mid Michigan Community College (MMCC) took up the challenge.

The odds were terrible. MMCC is a relatively small, rural college located in Harrison. Its chartered district is characterized by generational poverty and its associated social ills, including high unemployment and low educational attainment. In many cases, residents do not value higher education, arriving at our doors frightened and suspicious when life leaves no alternatives.

In addition, many residents are fixed-income retirees who have fled from high-tax areas of the state and are therefore resistant to tax increases. As a result, requests for additional tax support have been defeated eight times since the college was chartered 50 years ago. What was intended as one-third of our revenue stream has declined to a mere 9 percent. The ballot box seemed to be telling us quite clearly that a capital campaign would be doomed.

Similarly, the timing of the campaign could not have been worse. Michigan's economy, heavily reliant on the automotive industry, had not yet rebounded enough from the Great Recession to inspire optimism. Seeking jobs, people had left the state in droves. Property values plummeted, which caused state support of community colleges to shrink to 1998 levels. Further, several other nonprofit institutions in the region were involved in fundraising campaigns because their traditional revenue sources had dried up and philanthropy had become a more significant strategy.

Perhaps most daunting of all, the political landscape was challenging. Since its inception, Mid Michigan Community College has served a significant out-of-district population. In 1992 the college began offering classes in a large, converted office building in Mt. Pleasant, home to Central Michigan University. The secondary location quickly captured students' attention and, before long, more than 60 percent of MMCC's credits were generated at the Mt. Pleasant location.

The tension between the original, chartered district and the secondary site was ongoing, and often led to heated discussions. In-district residents wondered if their tax dollars were supporting an out-district location. Out-district residents questioned why they had to pay out-district tuition to attend a facility located in their city. Largely overshadowed by the university, MMCC was virtually unknown to business and social leaders in the Mt. Pleasant region. Yet our capital campaign was intended to provide significant support for building a new campus in the out-district location. While the financial rationale was sound, the logical explanation was complicated—not exactly an elevator speech.

As if these challenges weren't enough, the college had never conducted a capital campaign. The college foundation board and the college's governing board were focused on fundraising events and were squeamish about asking people for money. In fact, an attempt to launch a capital campaign six years earlier had been aborted before it began, lacking support from these same key board members. As a result, we didn't even know where to begin.

Then there was me, equally squeamish. President for six years at the time, of stalwart Scottish descent, I am a farmer's daughter who was reared to be self-sufficient and polite. Asking for money would have been a sign of weakness; inquiring about someone's finances would be a loathsome display of bad manners.

Even though I had been a college administrator for nearly 25 years, fundraising was not a skill set that I had developed—at least not sufficiently to overcome my childhood training. For years, I had avoided asking my acquaintances for money, even for great causes. My avoidance behavior was so great that I bought every ticket I was supposed to sell on behalf of civic organizations and gave them away. My knees turned to jelly, my heart pounded in my ears, and my tongue grew thick at the mere thought of asking relative strangers for large sums of money. In short, I was not a prime candidate to lead a major capital campaign.

Browning and Letterman would have had a field day counting the top ten reasons why our capital campaign wouldn't succeed, but we went forward anyway. Why? For me, there were two powerful and urgent reasons.

First, our capital plans were sound. We had spent years self-funding many sorely needed capital improvements on our Harrison campus to bring our technical labs, constructed in the 1970s, up to industry standards. Unifying all of our Mt. Pleasant operations onto one campus would be the final phase of creating operational efficiencies, effective services, and an environment conducive to teaching and learning. We had proven our fiscal responsibility by caring for our Harrison campus and by "making do" with crowded conditions and limited services at our Mt. Pleasant location. Now, the time had come for the college to take the next great leap forward in serving the entire region. It could not be done without finishing laboratory renovations on the Harrison campus and building a new campus in Mt. Pleasant, but funds were needed.

Second, I had great confidence in Matt Miller, our vice president responsible for college advancement. I knew he would commit to a campaign and make the personal sacrifices needed to see the campaign through until we reached our goal. (As an indicator that my confidence was not misplaced, he completed his doctorate while squarely in the throes of leading the college's first capital campaign.)

Even though Matt and I were passionate about our purpose, passion is not enough. From the beginning, we recognized the need for professional guidance. We gained board approval to seek consultants who would guide our efforts, but our plan was so tenuous at this point we easily could have been derailed. We wanted credible and competent campaign consultants who were flexible and who would work with our unique circumstances. Knowing that we would spend considerable time together, I also wanted consultants who were professional yet likeable, people who would be my confidants as well as my cheerleaders.

Fortunately, we found the ideal consultants by relying heavily on recommendations from other colleagues who had successfully used their services. Their initial feasibility study not only introduced the concept to several key leaders throughout the region, but also indicated that a $5 million campaign could succeed.

So we began. We probably weren't completely ready, but the important elements were in place.

The college's reputation was good. During the recession, we had demonstrated our responsiveness in providing retraining when the demands were almost unmanageably high. We had attended first to the capital needs of our chartered, in-district campus, and I had personally and broadly communicated the financial importance of our dual locations for several years.

Trust had been built with my governing board. They were not necessarily enthralled with the notion of a campaign, but they well understood my determination to reach goals and my tact in dealing with people. We had also slowly but intentionally begun formalizing our foundation board, seeking out a few new members who were brought aboard under newly created job descriptions that broadened and clarified expectations related to the full spectrum of fundraising.

Finally, during several years of intense lobbying, we had convinced the state legislature to approve funds for one-half of the most costly building we were proposing on the new campus. With these critical elements positioned, we felt we could learn the rest by doing. It's a good thing we didn't know what we didn't know!

Here is my advice from the trenches.

Start by developing your compelling story

If you are honest about the need for capital funds, you already know the facts. You know what needs to be built or renovated; you understand how this need aligns with your mission and strategic vision. Now you need to develop the persuasive and inspiring case for support. Taking the advice of our consultants, in developing our case for support we began with a very small group of individuals who were creative, forward looking, and deeply committed to the college. Led by our consultants, we brainstormed with this group about our points of pride, our distinctiveness in the marketplace and our vision for the future. The brainstorming helped us put more context around our building needs. Instead of brick and mortar, we began to connect our buildings vividly to the programs and services that would enrich our students' lives, invigorate our economy and contribute to a higher quality of life for everyone in our region. Our primary speaking points began to emerge.

At a later meeting, we invited a stakeholder group of loyal foundation, board and community members to help us refine the story and to serve as our sounding board. At this meeting, our consultants reviewed the speaking points we had developed and then asked me, unrehearsed, to share our unfolding case for support in my own words. As I began to describe the need for the capital projects, I choked and tears flooded my eyes. Later expressing my chagrin to our consultants, they responded wryly, "Can you do that every time?" Although they asked the question in jest, there was more than a kernel of truth in it. As a college president, I well understand that one of my primary roles is to motivate others, but telling this particular story required me to plumb new depths of my emotional reserves. I had to embrace this story both intellectually and emotionally; there couldn't be even a shred of doubt about our need for $5 million if we were to ask for that level of support in our complex, resource-strapped environment. My heartfelt words evoked my personal conviction, but even more important, we had begun to capture the attention of trustees and foundation members.

As we built the case for support together with our stakeholder group, saying the words aloud and questioning what each word meant, our thinking and conviction as a group became stronger. Trustees and foundation members who may have been either ambivalent or actively opposed began to rally around the notion of a $5 million capital campaign. We began to feel a shred of optimism. If the dam of resistance had been broken with this small but influential stakeholder group, perhaps a wider audience would respond enthusiastically to our request for support.

Over the next few weeks, we brought that story to life through a variety of multimedia communication tools. We were fortunate to have the requisite expertise in house, but even if you must outsource production of these tools, they are invaluable in reaching the diverse audiences you must influence.

If you are an introvert like me (according to Myers-Briggs), then you may suffer in this process. Picture this: I am standing in the middle of campus on a broiling hot day. A cameraman is taping me while our marketing director asks me questions about the campaign. Seeking spontaneity, my response is unrehearsed. Two interns hold reflecting screens on either side of me to erase shadows. Matt is just out of camera range, fanning me with a large piece of cardboard because I am visibly wilting in the heat. Students gawk; I am sure that I hear employees giggling. Our marketing director encourages me to just "act naturally." Sure. Of such humiliation are effective campaign videos made, but the process was worthwhile. With the production of each video, brochure, booklet, website or graphic, we requested feedback from our stakeholder group. Each time, they provided feedback and we altered our materials accordingly.

We could sense their commitment growing.

Design your campaign structure

With our consultants' expertise, we quickly laid out our timeline for a quiet phase in which we solicited major gifts, a public phase that created a broad sense of inclusion and an internal campaign that would engage college employees. We prioritized our approach, determining the order and the manner by which we would solicit contributions.

But we struggled with the campaign structure. Because of our lean staffing—and without any intention of hiring more staff for this campaign—we pictured a broad-based volunteer group, segmented by location and audience. We envisioned intensely involved community leaders chairing and directing activities for each segment. We approached several friends and supporters; we attempted to engage two or three community leaders who would have the credibility to take active leadership roles that would spur others to participate. People were attentive, they agreed with our mission and they ventured that our plans were solid. But they also politely yet firmly told us "no." Quite simply, we did not have a robust, long-term relationship with these leaders that would motivate them to take action. We found quickly that our volunteer base was not robust enough to rely on broad community support organized into a complex, hands-on structure.

We accepted the reality that the active work of the campaign would fall primarily to Matt, me and a small group of loyal supporters we called the "core team." The core team would serve a predominantly consultative role, helping us to identify and understand the relational needs and priorities of potential donors. Without having to commit to hands-on roles, we identified five honorary chairs who represented each sector of our geographical area and who lent great creditability to our campaign.

Because our campaign structure demanded a high level of involvement from Matt and me, we also had to set expectations for the board of trustees, faculty and staff, as well as our families. For at least a year, our roles would change dramatically. We would be available much less frequently in our offices on the Harrison campus. We would have to rely heavily on our direct reports to shoulder many of our traditional responsibilities. Our schedules would reflect the needs of the campaign, and any semblance of regular work hours would vanish. We would become much more outwardly focused. Our approach worked for us. You, too, must create a workable structure and approach fitted to your distinctive environment.

Attend to the details

Our consultants warned us, but it bears repeating: There are myriad details to sort out, and overlooking any of them can lead to embarrassment and donor angst, distrust or rejection. An easy-to-use database will be essential for tracking every interaction you have with each potential donor. Copious notes will be needed so that a select few campaign leaders can piece together donor preferences and priorities.

You must develop a fail-proof procedure for thanking potential donors for their time and interest in your projects and for following up appropriately. Your business processes must be such that donations are handled properly and donors' conditions of confidentiality or preferences for payments and pledge duration are respected.

You will need a method for coordinating schedules, meeting locations and amenities so that every gathering, large or small, on or off campus, showcases you and your college to the best advantage without mishap. If you intend to bestow naming rights to significant donors, you will need a policy and procedure for granting those rights. You will need protocols for volunteers and simple speaking points for key stakeholders. Consistent communication and coherent practices are required.

Other unanticipated details will emerge, and you must be flexible and adept at problem solving quickly. I soon found that Matt could turn a student lounge into an inviting reception area (complete with centerpieces) in just minutes if needed. We altered PowerPoint presentations while guests were walking up the sidewalk; we assigned roles to each other as equals. In short, you must rely on your advancement officer and trust each other's intuition. You must also be empowered to control the process in all of its infinite complexity, without bureaucratic constraints or hierarchical approval processes. After the initial launch of the campaign, our board of trustees was satisfied with monthly updates, allowing us to orchestrate the campaign as circumstances warranted.

Identify potential donors and define their capacity to contribute

The first part was fairly easy. We started with the college's long-time supporters, and asked a lot of questions. In fairly short order, a web of relationships began to emerge, from which we created a list of about 300 potential donors who could have a significant impact on the college. However, with flashbacks to my Scottish-tinged, self-reliant childhood, I cringed at the prospect of putting a dollar amount beside each name. To me, it seemed like a crass invasion of privacy.

Turns out, I was wrong. Based on publicly accessible information and a few gut-level hunches, we were able to quantify anticipated contributions and so brought clarity to the scope of work we had to complete to reach our goal. Along the way, we discovered that the greater objectivity we could bring to this project, the more feasible it became in our minds. We became less sensitive about the emotional aspects of the roles we were committed to play. For me, the Scottish "yuck factor" began to dissipate.

Start on friendly turf

Matt began the campaign by formally asking me for my personal contribution at a specific level. It was an important moment. He had to make a potentially uncomfortable ask. I was able to experience the emotional reaction of being asked. My response illustrated vividly one of our consultants' guiding principles: Never ask for an amount that is too low. Nevertheless, I took pity on Matt for his lowball request, doubling the amount of the pledge he had anticipated—and our campaign was launched! Next, we asked all board and foundation members to contribute. In individual meetings with each person, we saw tensions visibly subside when we made it crystal clear that we were seeking a contribution *at any level they wished.* Our stated goal was simply to receive a contribution from 100 percent of them.

Next, we sought contributions from my direct reports, making gentle suggestions for an appropriate level of contribution. This sequenced approach served two purposes. Campaign pledges from this friendly group—who all had a stake in the college—positioned us to communicate to others that the campaign enjoyed the total support of college leaders. It also gave us an approachable group of diverse personalities with whom we could safely practice our newly honed solicitation skills.

Next, we approached select external individuals with whom we had established long-term relationships. Their willing contributions and avid support were fodder for our efforts. In a very short time, we began to feel the power of our possibilities. We soon developed a rhythm that felt comfortable. Our story became effortless to tell, yet more powerful with each telling. We used each other's strengths and shored up our respective weaknesses. Matt was always much better at voicing the ask. I was better at telling the story with heartfelt emotion. Practice didn't make us perfect, because we treasured each donor's uniqueness. Yet by practicing, we were able to focus on the unique elements of developing the relationship without worrying about the details.

Use a 360-degree perspective

A critical few substantial donors will propel you to your goal, but you must create an unthreatening process for widespread participation. The ask should be at a level commensurate with the means of each donor. Everyone who has felt inspired by your college should be able to contribute meaningfully to the campaign at some level, and everyone should feel valued for their contribution. Our internal campaign was designed with those guiding principles in mind.

Internally, a team that represented each employee group created a series of fun activities that occurred over a relatively short period. The team had free rein to have fun—and they did. Administrators costumed as clowns sold candy, a good-natured administrator got dunked on a cold day, teams competed, and well-fought wars raged between departmental penny jars. Our stated goal was to have every employee return a pledge card at any value whatsoever. Every employee had a safe way to be involved, and we were thrilled to surpass the monetary goal we had designed into our campaign targets.

Similarly, we varied our approaches to suit the audience. We met privately with individuals and publicly with small groups. We convened at restaurants, golf courses and private homes. We learned more about our own operations as we conducted countless tours, answered hundreds of questions and helped prospective donors envision the new Mid Michigan Community College in the making. Every contact was prearranged thoughtfully, and our campaign consultants were ever-present as sounding boards and strategists in crafting a campaign that had widespread appeal.

Maintain your focus

None of this is about you. None of this is about your sore feet or scratchy throat when concluding your fifth tour and donor contact of the day. None of this is about the work yet to be done on your desk, about the thank you notes you still need to write, about your insecurities or about your ego. Instead, fundraising is about the college you love and the projects that are critical to serving your students and your community.

You will experience keen disappointments, when an anticipated check for $10,000 turns out to be for $100. You will experience awkwardness, when a board member expresses doubt or a potential donor reminds you about his or her disappointment in a college program, service or initiative. You will learn of wrongs that occurred decades ago, but you will be bolstered by stories of transformation wrought by your expert, caring instructors and staff. Realize, also, that your campaign is not solely about the funding. At its core, your campaign creates awareness of your college's impact on the community and builds relationships that will endure and sustain your institution for years to come. Don't be distracted by the irrelevancies that will inevitably occur.

Commit your whole self

Campaign champions need to realize that a capital campaign requires your head, your hand and your heart. You must engage your intellect to objectively design a campaign and organize for results. You must engage your hand because you must take an involved, hands-on approach to meeting donors and to spending the quality time needed to discover their interests.

Perhaps most of all, a campaign takes your heart, as you delve deeply within yourself to communicate the need with passion and conviction, whether you are telling your story for the first time or the hundredth time. You cannot successfully lead a campaign if you are only superficially or intermittently interested.

Furthermore, a successful campaign demands the college president's undivided attention. Although a great deal of development work can be completed by other skilled advancement personnel—Matt and his staff directed and organized every aspect of the campaign—the president's presence and conviction lend the credibility that is vital to realize significant support.

Celebrate and sustain

Rejoice in victories both large and small as they occur. Let your boards and your college community enjoy your progress with you. Communicate broadly as you come closer to realizing your goal. Show your donors the fruits of their generosity when your projects are completed. Continue to tell donors powerful stories about the lives that have been touched and transformed as a result of their philanthropy. Determine ways in which campaign champions can continue meaningful involvement with your college, on advisory committees or foundation boards, in fundraising events or volunteer services, as adjuncts, student mentors or tutors. Cherish your cadre of supporters.

A capital campaign is merely the first step in a long-lasting association if you continue nurturing the relationship.

The results and rewards

We raised $5 million in a little over 18 months. Our new Center for Imaging Studies on the Harrison campus now provides a health care setting that encourages radiography students to develop both job competencies and soft skills. We have a unified, new campus in Mt. Pleasant. The spacious new buildings, student gathering areas, learning environments and laboratories that reflect industry standards exceed my lofty expectations. I experience a satisfying thrill walking through these buildings, but echoing in the corridors, classrooms, laboratories and communities I hear the energy of our students, the excitement of community members, the self-worth growing in trained workers, the clang of flourishing businesses and the generosity of our donors. I envision their pride in our college.

The funds raised were vital to creating appropriate learning spaces, but the campaign accomplished so much more than addressing our facility needs. Our capacity to raise funds has grown exponentially. Success breeds confidence. Vital systems and processes are in place. We have developed relationships with influential community leaders who will help garner support in the future, because they heard our story, believe in our mission and value Mid Michigan Community College. Only 18 months previously, many of our donors did not know who we were; now they are invested in who we will become. We began with trepidation, counting all the ways our campaign could fail. With expert guidance, careful planning and execution, dedication and commitment, we can count our supporters. Begin counting yours.

Chapter 14

GETTING TO THE NEXT LEVEL

What Does It Take?

By William T. Scroggins

Most community college foundations are doing good work, but few could be considered high functioning. How can these foundations—regardless of their age, size or budget—move to the next level? Adequate staffing and resources are, of course, a factor, but it's the college president who plays the key role, serving as the catalyst, architect and cheerleader to get the college's foundation to the next level.

So where do you start?

Let's assume you have just taken an in-depth look at your college foundation: endowment level, annual fund receipts, event costs and revenue, staffing levels and qualifications, board of directors' resumes and yearly contribution levels, donor list and giving history, and perhaps an audit or two. You probably did not find what you had hoped. But what DID you hope to find?

Step back for a moment. Focus on two questions. What would you realistically expect from the existing structure and function of your foundation? What is your vision of a high-performing foundation that would support your goals for the institution? Your vision for the foundation must incorporate today's reality, tomorrow's goal and a path to connect the two.

Measuring foundation performance

Let's start with what we are going to measure. What does a foundation contribute to a college? First, of course, is revenue. That revenue is scrounged for and ladled out in three flavors. Foundations facilitate *donations for student scholarships*, best done with endowment gifts but also achievable through annual pledges. Some foundations raise *income to support their internal operations*. Ideally it is best if the foundation can support its own operations, like most four-year foundations do, but because of their size and limited assets, most community college foundations are funded all or in part by the college they serve. Finally, foundations receive donations that directly *support the work of the college.* Typically those donations fund projects, equipment or staffing. Project revenue may arrive through designated gifts or optimally through annual distribution of income earned from the corpus of the endowment. So metric number one for foundation performance is money—cash (the folding kind).

Not long after my arrival at one of the colleges I served, I started the in-depth look mentioned earlier. In reviewing financial reports, I found the various revenue streams to be so mixed up that I could not figure out how much the foundation was actually receiving in these three areas. Further complicating matters was the booking of college in-kind support (mostly two salaries of foundation personnel) as revenue. It looked like the foundation was taking in quite a bit, but a closer look showed that foundation operating bills were being paid out of the corpus of the endowment, which was almost gone. Not good.

The solution (at least to the accounting issue)? We contracted with an accountant who specialized in nonprofits, brought him to the board of directors meetings for three consecutive sessions, and (a) reformatted the books to tag each type of revenue and expenditure, (b) produced report formats that honestly reflected revenues and expenditures related to the budget and (c) made sure that the board of directors could understand, and give direction from, the resulting reports.

Beyond accounting, clear and consistent gift acceptance policies are essential to a growing foundation. At another institution where I worked, unclear policies and lack of interdepartmental coordination resulted in sloppy handling of an in-kind donation. The

Evaluate foundations by

- Revenue and expenditures
  - » Scholarships
  - » Operations
  - » Designated gifts
- Endowment size
  - » Restricted
  - » Unrestricted
- Major gift pledges
- Advancement contribution

issue stemmed from a piece of equipment that was accepted by the foundation, inventoried by the administration and then sold as surplus by another department—with no communication among the three entities. The value of the write-off was determined by the foundation through certification by an industry professional (at what turned out to be a rather elevated value), and then the equipment was sold to that same certifying professional (although the department was unaware of this). We found out later that the certifying professional/buyer was a friend of the donor. Wrong on so many levels. Needless to say, our process was revised. Word to the wise: get all college parties in the room when foundation gift, revenue and expenditure processes are set up or revised.

Another important performance metric is endowment. The dollar amount in the endowment, both restricted and unrestricted, is as important as the annual cash spent by the foundation on college and student support. It is a measure of the foundation's future investment in the college and the second metric by which to evaluate the foundation.

Most endowments are built through major gifts rather than by annual giving. Thus a significant third measure of foundation performance is pledges for future major gifts. Planned giving for major gifts cannot be quantified as precisely as cash in the bank, but reporting those outcomes is an essential measure of foundation accomplishments.

Money, money, money. Is that all there is to a foundation? Absolutely not. Foundations are central to the overall advancement of the college. What does *advancement* mean? In this context, it refers to fundraising, public relations and related activities.

As a college president, I spend a major portion of my time building and maintaining relationships with business leaders, elected representatives, government officials, community organizations, service clubs, other educational institutions and, of course, those at the college. My major purpose in engaging these people is usually not philanthropy, but it is almost always one of the elements of that contact.

For example, I talk about our fabulous new Pathways to Transfer program that accelerates students through the math sequence, and I do not forget to mention that we have limited funds to expand this successful initiative. When I see a spark of interest in the [fill in the blank: business/vendor/partner], I produce a "leave behind" brochure that has been developed in partnership among the foundation executive director, the marketing director, and the dean of science and math. In promoting the college through relationship building, I am also looking for ways to promote the foundation. And vice versa. At foundation events, I look for ways to promote the college. That's advancement.

Getting the most from the existing foundation structure

What are the capabilities of existing foundation personnel, current fundraising strategies and projects, and sitting members of the foundation board of directors? Following are a few hints and a couple of stories, but please note that individual situations vary widely.

Let's start with you, the college president. You are the architect, the visionary, the motivator, the carrot and stick; and, titles aside, you are the chief fundraising officer.

Consequently, take inventory of your knowledge, skills and experience. We all could use more of each of those, so find some training, workshop or conference that seems to fit what you need to refresh, grow and get energized about being the catalyst for moving your foundation to the next level.

Now, for the foundation executive director: That person needs to be skilled and experienced in the profession of nonprofit fundraising. Skills include organizational leadership (running a small, underfunded, ill-staffed organization), vision (equal parts rose-colored glasses and blindfolds), and inspiring written and oral communication (think of the range from sincere Hallmark cards to motivational speeches). What this person cannot be is low energy, boring or thin skinned. Is the executive director licking stamps and answering phones? If so, that time is not being spent building relationships, developing prospects and making asks. This is a profession that is a real calling. It is not a job to be reassigned to that person on your staff who has not succeeded at his or her last three assignments.

Support staff are equally important. Skills should match the organization's strategy. Doing events? Have event-planning skills. Managing a prospect database? Have computer skills. Doing alumni contacts, call backs, and board care and feeding? Have people skills. Seems obvious, but you would be surprised how often personnel can be a speed bump for a foundation trying to get revved up.

Are the foundation staff doing foundation work? Really? One of the colleges at which I worked had one full-time executive director and one full-time support staff. Fundraising produced a balance among scholarships, operations and college projects, and the endowment was growing steadily. The executive director was motivated to get to the next level, and part of the in-depth look was at staff. The problem? Scholarship applications, evaluations, awards and recognition all were handled inside the foundation. Those activities consumed a large part of the support staff member's time. Solution? I moved the mechanics of the scholarship process inside the financial aid office. But then the skills set of the foundation staff member did not match the work of the revved-up foundation. Solution? I moved the staff member to financial aid as well, and we hired a new staffer for the foundation—with skills to match the new agenda. Both the financial aid office and the staffer were happy with the new arrangement.

Does the make-up of the board of directors match the work of the foundation as it is presently conducted? If the work is "scholarships, socials and saccharine," then you need lightweights on your board of directors. If the work is relationship building, lead development and fundraising, then your board of directors needs people of means and influence.

Vision of the "Next Level" foundation

Plenty of community colleges (and college presidents) are just fine with passing through funds for scholarships and promoting the college through galas and hall-of-fame celebrations. If you want to conduct serious fundraising, though, foundation leadership, staffing and projects as well as the foundation's board of directors should match the vision you have as CEO.

Think of the qualities and characteristics you need as if it were an online dating site like Match.com. Which of the following are important to taking your foundation to the next level?

- ☐ CEO is chief fundraiser
- ☐ Highly qualified director
- ☐ 3+ skilled support staff
- ☐ Office space: generous
- ☐ Office space: campus central
- ☐ Alumni database: contact info
- ☐ Alumni database: gift history
- ☐ Alumni database: wealth scores
- ☐ Alumni database: major interests
- ☐ Alumni database: campus connection
- ☐ Annual vendor donor event
- ☐ All events: break even+ friend-raisers
- ☐ "Give and get" board of directors
- ☐ Seven- or eight-figure endowment
- ☐ Six-figure annual fund
- ☐ Effective planned giving
- ☐ A+ scholarship office
- ☐ 50%+ employee giving
- ☐ A+ advisory committee
- ☐ Support from marketing
- ☐ Support from finance office
- ☐ Support from IT

Did you check them all? If so, you have a vision for the "Next Level" foundation. Now connect your existing foundation with your "Next Level" foundation by developing a strategic pathway.

Strategies aside, sometimes fundraising is just dumb luck. You're doing the right thing and don't even know it. A few years ago at another college, I was out in the community proselytizing for the public to vote for a facilities bond. Two of the successful programs I was citing were the nursing school and the fire academy. You know the routine: the helping professions, high percentage educated in community colleges, great completion rate, grads stay in the community, heart-tugging stories. In the audience was an elderly lady who previously had a stroke, was quickly revived by a firefighter and then served lovingly by a nurse in the hospital. Both the firefighter and the nurse had been educated at my college. Result: an unsolicited, unrestricted seven-figure gift. Telling the story and asking for financial help does get results, sometimes in unexpected ways. I was asking for bond money and got a philanthropic donation. And the bond passed, too!

Ensuring talented and dedicated foundation leadership

In your role as the chief fundraiser, you need a competent foundation executive director. In my experience, six skills are important for this position: (a) passion for fundraising, (b) engaging personality and people skills, (c) existing relationships in the community served by the college, (d) experience in fundraising, (e) knowledge of higher education and (f) organizational skills. These are in order of importance. You cannot teach passion or personality. Knowledge of the community and relationships within it take time but can be developed, as can fundraising experience. However, lack of these at the outset will affect your timeline for getting to the next level. The ins and outs of higher education can be picked up with some mentoring, and organizational skills can be learned. One of the challenges of hiring an executive director is that passion and personality are hard to glean from a resume.

My advice is to make the job announcement attractive to a wide range of applicants and then interview many more than is typical—and focus the interview on passion and personality. Finally, do not scrimp on compensation. To get the skills you need, in most cases you will be stealing a person from an existing high-functioning organization. Have a salary schedule with several high-end steps. You are going to ask this person to grow and advance the foundation to the next level, and the compensation should grow commensurate with the increasing responsibilities of the executive director as the foundation expands.

At one of the colleges I led, I inherited a foundation executive director who was low on three key skills. After getting to know him, it was apparent that the deficit in people skills and in leading the organization stemmed from low self-esteem. This was a guy with talent who had overcome a lot in his life. He wanted in the worst way to get that foundation to the next level. So, with his approval, I introduced him to a mentor I knew well and trusted implicitly. Beyond my introduction, I had no involvement in their mentoring relationship. After a year, the change was noticeable: He was much more confident in dealing with others and thus was able to be properly assertive in leading the foundation organization. But number one, his passion for fundraising was still at low ebb. So I did my best to be the source of enthusiasm, energy and passion for our fundraising efforts. And we did get to the next level—and he did continue to grow as an educational professional. Eventually, he expressed interest in serving the college in a broader role and was selected for a more responsible position in the organization.

The opportunity thus presented itself to select a new foundation executive director with passion, personality and experience—who inherited a well-run organization smoothly transferred from the previous executive director. The point? Those six skills must be available to the foundation through its leaders: executive director, college president and, in some cases, the president of the foundation board.

It is hard to underestimate the importance of the foundation executive director, particularly in the climb to the next level. Transforming an organization is challenging at best and depressing and deflating at worst. As CEO, be prepared to buoy up spirits, ensure job security, affirm professionalism, give advice and solve problems.

Getting the college team on board

How does the CEO lead the transition of the foundation to the next level? You must have—or must create—a mandate: a call to action, marching orders. Why do you need a mandate? First, getting to the next level takes time, and folks at the college will get impatient, particularly if you did not start with a sense of purpose, passion and power. Getting to the next level takes a minimum of three years.

Second, getting from "scholarships, socials and saccharine" to "Next Level" takes resources. You will need to direct or redirect resources as an investment to produce future returns. Regardless of where we are in the rollercoaster of the economy, it is a challenge to invest money with the hope of future return when present needs are so urgent. Viewing philanthropy as a mandate establishes a basis for investment in building the foundation.

Third, getting to the next level takes cooperation from other units on the campus—willing cooperation. It is *you* who must frame this compelling mandate and bring others along.

You'll need the blessing of the governing board—your "bosses." I have found four action steps to be useful for engaging the governing board members in the mandate to improve the foundation:

- Philanthropy should be in the CEO's job description and annual evaluation. This creates three opportunities for constructive dialogue between you and the governing board. Upon being hired, you (as CEO) and the board can discuss the importance of philanthropy and set mutual goals. Each year, in your self-evaluation, you can emphasize not only recent accomplishments in philanthropy but also your mandate—and strategy—for moving the foundation to the next level. Finally, in discussing the governing board's evaluation of your performance, the dialogue can reaffirm the mutual commitment of the board and president to the necessary and often challenging steps required to advance the foundation.
- At least one of the governing board members should be on the foundation board of directors. This demonstrates visibly the support of the governing board for the foundation and allows that governing board member to be intimately familiar with the importance of investing in the foundation. This governing board member should be cultivated as an ally for you as CEO, since decisions for staffing, facilities and financial support come before the governing board.
- The foundation executive director should make reports to the governing board at its regular meetings. This report should concisely summarize progress on building the foundation, on contacts and events, and on the actual dollar value of donations. Such reports give consistent high visibility to the executive director, signal to college staff and the community the importance of the foundation,

and build a strong relationship between the executive director and members of the governing board.

- Governing board members should be asked to take a personal role in identifying potential donors and perhaps using their relationships to introduce potential donors to the foundation. Invite each governing board member to meet with you and the foundation executive director to discuss how he or she can establish and meet a "give and get" goal.

At one of the colleges at which I served as president, it was clear in my job interview that the governing board wanted my leadership in philanthropy. Good, I thought. When I stepped on the campus, I discovered that the board—not just one but the whole passel of them—had issues with the current foundation executive director. Investigating, I found that her job description had been approved by the foundation board but not by the board of trustees, that she was not in regular communication with the trustees and that she had neither cultivated new donors nor maintained contact with existing donors. The board of trustees wanted to directly evaluate her and set donation goals for the foundation.

So I used one of my "honeymoon cards" as a new hire to get the trustees to let me handle the situation. After some investigation to get my facts straight, I met with the executive director and let her know that it was my intention to conduct her overdue evaluation, establish a regular role for her to report at monthly trustee meetings, and review her role with donors and potential donors. I offered my assistance to achieve these outcomes but left no doubt about the desired outcomes. Within two months she had accepted a job at another foundation. And I had a mandate from the board of trustees to get the foundation to the next level.

It is important that key units on campus—marketing and the business office, in particular—be on board with giving direct support to the foundation. As CEO you have several roles in making this happen: matchmaker, traffic cop and coach.

Marketing and the foundation have a natural shared mission in promoting the advancement of the college. Remember that advancement is one of the metrics on which the foundation is evaluated. Again, this is a two-way street. Foundation events and outreach should use the messaging and branding developed by marketing. Marketing materials and messages should both build the image of the college and celebrate the achievements of the foundation. As matchmaker, you can promote this mutual mission by having marketing and the foundation work as a team when events, materials and messages are produced. As traffic cop, you can ensure that projects you review and approve have input from both units. As coach, you can work with the directors of both units to help them identify and value overlapping tasks.

The business office and the foundation must work together as foundation revenue is booked and distributed, and when the college and the foundation are audited. It is important that fiscal processes, forms and approvals are mutually agreed upon between the two units. Particularly important is the handling of money collected at fundraising events.

Transforming college processes that have an extensive history is always a challenge. Add money to the equation and you have a combustible mixture. At one of the colleges I served, the Culture Fair was a long-standing event, with music, dancing, costumes, displays of artifacts from around the world and booths selling delectable ethnic goodies. The foundation supported the event by soliciting monetary donations for scholarships, by accepting in-kind donations, and by booking the food sales income and paying related bills.

One day we received an audit exception for lack of controls in handling the cash from the food sales. The business office started down the path of concocting rules, forms and monitoring devices. The groups that ran the Culture Fair lamented the demise of the event from the heavy burden of red tape. In I stepped as the traffic cop. The result: Each food booth group filled out a simple form selecting one of two cash-handling systems. Option 1 was a cash box checked out from and returned to the Bursar's Office. Option 2 was to have patrons buy tickets from the Bursar's Office redeemable for food items. The business office had their cash accountability, and the foundation had a nice record of revenues.

In addition to the "partner" units on campus, the foundation must establish productive relationships with other departments and individuals on campus. These partnerships have three potential positive outcomes: blue-ribbon needs lists to promote to potential donors, departmental relationships with alumni and other potential donors, and direct employee giving to the foundation.

A foundation's database should include a donor or prospect's area of giving interest. With this information the foundation can show how high-performing the college happens to be in this area and share needs of the program or service that is of interest to the donor. It is important that the executive director develop relationships with key managers around campus. Assure each manager that the foundation will work with the department to craft outreach to alumni and business partners in a way that maintains and enhances existing relationships. If you start with departments that already have a good relationship with the foundation, others can develop confidence in foundation activities. There is no better message than to share how foundation outreach has resulted in direct fiscal support to departments on campus.

It has been my experience that employee-giving campaigns are more effective in later stages of foundation growth and development. Employees need confidence that the foundation is worthy of their donations. We see the deep and extensive needs of our students and want to be sure that our precious donations produce results. Here are three things to keep in mind: leader gifts, recognition and feedback. Employees want to see that trustees and senior management are giving, so recognize them publicly. Employee donors appreciate knowing that their gifts make a difference through feedback such as letters from student recipients or donor plaques displayed prominently.

Establishing a strategic timeline

If you want to take your foundation from "scholarships, socials and saccharine" to "advancement, enhancement and endowment," plan on three years for the transition.

Year 1: Inspiration, information, reformation

- *Start talking.* Develop and deliver a clear, concise inspirational message to share your vision about the future of the foundation. Remember, you are creating a mandate! Tell everyone: trustees, community members, the media and your college (especially marketing, finance and IT). You are building energy and creating buy-in for what will come later: the ask.
- *Take stock.* Evaluate what you have, compare with what you need and then develop a plan. Use existing college evaluation, planning and budgeting processes. Don't make the foundation look like it's separate from the college; include the foundation director on your cabinet.
- *Hire a great executive director.* Then hire staff with the right skills for your vision.
- *Build that great database.* Start with current donors. Pull together everything you know about them. Extract information on alumni from your database(s). Buy software: a donor management system with all the bells and whistles.
- *Build relationships with current donors.* Call them. Visit them. Bring them on campus. Use this experience to develop a solid donor care-and-feeding process.
- *Restructure the organization.* Not the whole thing yet, just the first step in year 1: policies and processes. Work with your existing foundation board of directors to evaluate and rewrite (as needed) the foundation standards and practices to reflect the new, nimble, responsive organization of your vision. Use this experience as a first step to changing the board, but don't do a wholesale swap-out the first year.

Year 2: Boards, budgets and buddies

- *Transition the board.* Begin with directors who "get it." Have them be champions of the "Next Level" foundation. Talk to each director individually about his or her role: some will step up, some will step out and some will step aside when their term is up. Recruit new directors of affluence and influence. Don't be shy about "give and get." When you get to a critical mass of existing champions and new blood, have the board of directors adopt a formal standard for annual director donations and fundraising. Although this is a Year 2 project, be patient as this work may extend into Year 3.
- *Build relationships.* Get on the community circuit with your executive director. Send handwritten follow-up notes to those with whom you meet. Have your executive director visit campus administrators and faculty: Mine them for funding needs, and look for opportunities for campus projects to fund. Set up one-on-one meetings for you and the executive director with trustees and mine them for contacts, too. Now is the time to start alumni solicitations for the annual fund. Keep a

major prospects list and work the list. Be sure to include the vendors with whom your college does business. Set up a vendor appreciation event to kick this off. Have your staff who work with each vendor be a major part of the event. Market the foundation by creating an advancement strategy with the buy-in and collaboration of your marketing department.

- *Cover the operating budget shortfalls.* During the three-year plan, commit to covering foundation operating budget shortfalls. By Year 2 you should be paying from your college budget, at most, the cost of your two foundation managers. Two good reasons to keep these folks on your college payroll: It's a sign of support and faith in their work *and* it removes the pressure on them to fundraise for their own salaries. The foundation operating budget—the "nut" beyond your two managers—should be covered by (a) no more than two major annual fundraising events, (b) board of director "gives" of at least $2,500 each year, (c) annual fund donations and (d) unrestricted donations from the President's Circle or whatever you choose to call "selling" direct access to the president.
- *Start asking!* Develop a comprehensive solicitation strategy, recognizing that nothing is more effective than a personal request for support—or a personal introduction. This includes asking your board members, and having them ask others. At one of the colleges I served, the director was a widow who owned five successful local companies built by her late husband. She was socially connected and had been the "event guru" of our foundation—and she gave generously herself each year. No one had ever asked her about her connections with others of means in the community. Turns out she was a great stringer who brought in several large pledges and major gifts. She stepped up. You don't get if you don't ask.

Year 3: MAGIC (Major gifts, Annual fund, Give and get, Investment return, president's Circle)

- *Build the annual fund, alumni association and employee giving.* By Year 3 you should have significant responses from your annual solicitations. You should have a functioning alumni association. Your annual employee-giving campaign is yielding initial good results. Your marketing folks are producing great advancement materials that promote the foundation; IT has your website humming; and finance has your back on budget, revenues, expenditures, audits, taxes, and all that stuff that foundation executive directors hate to do and were not hired to do. You have celebration events for alumni, employee supporters, vendor supporters, scholarship recipients and their donors, and President's Circle major donors.
- *Focus on major gifts and pledges.* With all the basic stuff humming along, it's time to reach for the brass ring. Work that prospect list to secure major gifts. Remember that you need wealth scores, a stringer connection to the college, and donor proclivities with fundable college projects or naming opportunities to match. Bring together a key group of people to work on major gifts. Define roles. A typical

team for each potential major donor includes the stringer (the individual with the personal or professional connection with the donor), the campus person who can best talk about the project, the tax adviser (who knows how to structure gifts) and the closer (the person who will make the ask—typically you or the executive director). Be patient. Major gifts often result from gradual increases in giving over an extended period of time. Be ready with your team, since opportunities can arise at the drop of a hat. Publicize giving opportunities—funded projects and naming opportunities. Don't be shy about including these in your publications and other communications.

- *All on board with "give and get."* By the end of Year 3, all the board of directors are giving at least $2,500 each year and getting at least $2,500 in donations. Your executive director should be meeting regularly with all directors—working especially closely with those who need help with give and get. Have the executive director give you a status report on these activities at least quarterly. Step in and help when necessary. Celebrate that annual achievement of 100-percent give and get.
- *Create an investment policy.* Your board of directors should have an investment committee and an investment policy. This policy should be reviewed regularly to adjust the mix of investments. Your policy should address reinvestment and expenditures, including protection of the corpus of your endowments.
- *Ramp up the President's Circle.* In Years 1 and 2, you may not have sufficient major donors to justify a full President's Circle. You have been giving these folks special attention, but an annual event with three or four participants is anticlimactic. By Year 3, you should have a half-dozen or so donors at the top two rungs of your President's Circle pyramid. So hold an event at which you report on emerging issues in higher education (or some other high-powered topic) and get their input. Remember, access to you is an asset that has value.
- *Keep asking!* Ask others to give; ask others to help ask. It's worth repeating: You don't get if you don't ask.

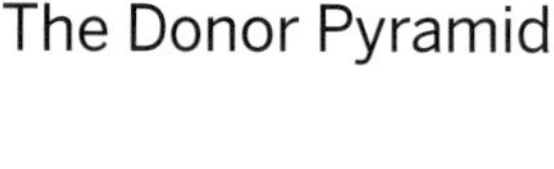

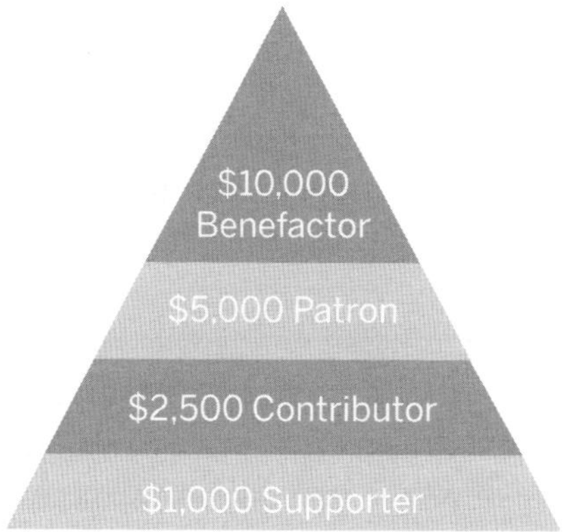

Managing transitions: staff, board, financials, data, training, outreach

Managing change is a central role of every college president. As the chief fundraiser, your job is to transition the foundation to the next level. Yes, your executive director is a partner in this reinvention project, but the campus and the community need to see you at the helm. Give personal attention to molding the fundraising staff to your vision, and don't hesitate to make personnel changes.

Changing foundation board directors can be delicate. Find other significant roles for those who are assets to the college but not of means or influence. Appoint them to an advisory committee, get them to help with the alumni association or have them help with events. And keep in touch with them. Mine your contacts and those of your senior staff and board of trustees for foundation director candidates. Make sure they are of means and influence, and let them know of your high standards going in. Also, get their personal commitment to "give and get."

Get the rest of your team—especially marketing, finance and IT—on board with supporting the foundation. Be direct in facing the challenge of getting these folks to invest their hearts and minds. (a) They won't immediately see the value of this work, so convince them. (b) They are busy with other work, so be sure that foundation tasks are prioritized as a part of their regular agenda—and give them permission to say no to other projects. (c) They will need to join foundation staff meetings periodically, so be sure they understand that they can contribute more than just their work products. Be sure to share credit for foundation success with these support units as well.

Emphasize training of foundation staff, foundation board members and support team members. Fundraising is a skill, an advanced profession. Remember that most team members have not had training in philanthropy, and probably fear it.

As college president, provide a clear, consistent message on philanthropy. Look for every opportunity to build fundraising into the fabric of the college.

Here's a story to illustrate: One of my responsibilities is to review and approve architectural plans for new and remodeled buildings. During this process, I look for simple adjustments that might add value to our advancement agenda. Our new business building design included expanded space for our Hospitality Management and Culinary Arts programs, including a functioning commercial restaurant. It was in a good location with excellent customer access on the bottom floor of the three-building complex. A second-floor walkway connected adjacent buildings, forming a breezeway adjacent to the restaurant. With minor modifications, that area became a covered gathering area with a raised platform stage that will function as an expanded outdoor service area when we use the restaurant for college public activities, including philanthropic events. We already have several such locations on campus and use them regularly for VIP gatherings. A similar area, an atrium in our design technology building, hosts a scholarship fundraising event put on annually by our Astronomy Department that raises thousands of dollars—and showcases that wonderful program. Soon we will have a similar location for such events connected to our Business Division.

Patience, persistence, advocacy and midstream adjustments

If we expect to have work that is predictable, to be filled with serenity and to receive endless positive feedback, we are in the wrong profession. Foundations are but one more area in which we have influence but not control, insight but not certainty, and satisfaction from incremental gains rather than from fundamental transformations. So be patient, be persistent, never flag in your advocacy and make course corrections as needed. Remember that the gold standard—major gifts—likely will not be realized until long after you are gone. But those who follow you will be grateful.

The role you play and the tone you set will make the difference.

To illustrate: One day our foundation director and assistant director stopped by my office. With long faces and downcast expressions, they related criticisms they had endured about a recent event that had been a partnership with another unit on campus: "They just want their old way of doing things!" "They think we are trying to take over!" "They won't let us be partners in planning the event!"

So, as an old classroom teacher, I began using the Socratic method. Were you able to attend the planning meeting? "Well, yes, but we were in the back, not on the agenda, and had to wait to speak." Were you able to make changes in the program? "Well, yes, but so much more could be done!" Did the event make more money? "Well, yes, but it could have made so much MORE!" My responses: So you participated and improved both the program and the outcome. You also gained credibility with the group. You also now understand how they work, and have time to refine your suggestions for the next iteration of the program. Those results alone are incredibly valuable outcomes. Change is slow at times, so recognize your successes.

When leaving my office, the executive director commented, "When I come to your office with seemingly insurmountable barriers, I always leave feeling reaffirmed and hopeful. How do you do that?"

Well, my fellow CEOs, that's our job, isn't it?

Section IV

COMMUNICATIONS & ENGAGEMENT

Chapter 15

KIRKWOOD'S ALUMNI & FRIENDS

The Power of Connecting

By Mick Starcevich

It was the end of a long day in an unfamiliar place. I was traveling with one of Kirkwood Community College's international service learning groups, and we had spent the day building houses in an impoverished village in Guatemala. After 12 hours of the hardest physical work I've ever done, it was a relief to relax with a group of Kirkwood students and faculty at a local restaurant. We were keenly aware of how far we'd traveled and how far we were from home. Imagine my surprise when a young woman across the room saw our Kirkwood shirts, approached our table with a big smile and said, "I know where you're from! I graduated from Kirkwood, and now I'm a first-grade teacher in Antigua!" What a reminder that our alumni really are everywhere.

Why have a community college alumni program?

When other presidents ask me why Kirkwood supports an alumni program, I say, "Why wouldn't we?" With more than 70,000 alumni across the world (and over 80 percent living right here in our seven-county service region), our alumni are our closest friends and our best ambassadors. Why wouldn't we take advantage of a built-in base of satisfied customers to spread the message about Kirkwood?

Like many community colleges, Kirkwood did not have a well-established alumni program when I became president in 2005. Although there had been short-lived attempts to connect with alumni throughout the college's history, there was no consistent effort in place and no real program. Our foundation, the typical host for a college alumni program, was successful at raising funds through major and planned giving but was not particularly interested in launching an alumni program. The prevailing wisdom among community college foundations at the time was that alumni wouldn't become donors, so the return on investment wouldn't justify sponsoring an alumni program.

Also, like many colleges still do, Kirkwood had convinced itself—wrongly—that our students transfer their allegiance to four-year institutions if they move on. As we learned, our former students value us, support us and want to give back. We just had not asked.

Our first big alumni gift

In 2005 an alumnus named Michael Gould called the foundation office and inquired about establishing an endowed scholarship to honor a former professor. It was late on a Friday afternoon, and he reached a brand-new foundation employee who scrambled to answer his questions. He made the gift, and he liked seeing his scholarship at work.

Just a year later, Michael and his wife, Jan, gave Kirkwood our first $1 million donation, establishing another endowed scholarship for students with financial need. We named our new recreation center in his honor, and he has since become one of our closest friends. We all noticed that at least one alumnus had the interest and capacity to give—might there be more?

As a new college president in 2005 (my background was as a K–12 superintendent), I was faced with many competing priorities. To bring them into focus, I launched a planning process in 2006 called the Kirkwood Futures Initiative (KFI). One KFI strategy was to "establish an alumni community-building model." I knew embedding the alumni program as a part of the institution's strategic plan would be critically important to building college support for the effort.

A positive force

On an instinctive level, it has always made sense to me for Kirkwood to connect with our alumni, not just because of the potential for alumni giving, but also because a look at the big picture shows so many benefits. Kirkwood's alumni make up a significant percentage of our service-region population. They vote when we have levies and bond issues on the ballot, they are lifelong learners who return for credit and noncredit classes, they recommend Kirkwood to their families and neighbors, and they shape community perception about our institution. When we keep our alumni engaged and happy, they are a powerful and positive public relations force.

Early decisions

We made several key decisions when launching our alumni initiative. The foundation stepped up as the natural entity to house the program, taking the initial steps in 2007 to import student records into the foundation database and implement a new online alumni networking platform paid for by foundation board–designated funds.

Just after that, a new foundation executive director, Kathy Hall, was appointed. Her background in nonprofit community leadership led her to champion the public relations potential of the alumni program. After some initial staff transition, Kathy asked Jody Donaldson, the foundation's talented scholarship director, to take on the additional responsibility of leading the alumni program. A Kirkwood alumna herself, Jody has proven to be a passionate and inspired choice. Her consistent leadership since 2008 has been a key factor in the success of Kirkwood's Alumni & Friends.

One of Jody's first steps was to create an internal, cross-departmental college steering committee to help develop the alumni program. With representatives from student affairs, career services, marketing, admissions, continuing education and several academic departments, the group knew they wanted to create an alumni network, but they didn't know what it should look like. Should it be a dues-paying, members-only organization? Should it be modeled after the alumni associations of four-year colleges? Would it be structured as a board or as an advisory committee? Most of all, what kind of connection did our alumni want? I knew we had critical decisions to make, and I didn't want them to be based on speculation. We needed help.

In late 2008 I offered college funding for the "Alumni Relationship Study," a survey professionally conducted by Epley Research & Consulting. The internal steering committee worked with Epley to develop the questions for a qualitative survey designed to answer the question "What is the best way for us to reach a deeper understanding of our alumni?" Conducted over several months, the study profiled 40 alumni, evenly divided between recent graduates and graduates from more than 11 years ago. They were asked what they found at Kirkwood, how they see Kirkwood today, and how they would engage with and support the college today.

The responses of those surveyed were encouraging. In general, they described overwhelmingly positive experiences with Kirkwood, an interest in staying abreast of news and changes in the institution, and a strong willingness to recommend Kirkwood to others. The key difference in the responses of Kirkwood alumni and the alumni of four-year schools is that Kirkwood alumni view themselves as satisfied consumers of education, but they don't have a built-in sense of obligation to support the institution. This helped set our expectation that the initial value of the alumni program would be primarily in its public relations benefit.

Alumni Leadership Council

After the survey was completed and the results reviewed by the internal team and my cabinet, Jody formed an external Alumni Leadership Council. Structured as an advisory committee, the council was established in 2009 with 21 community members serving three-year terms. We decided early on that this group would represent all alumni and friends, and that we would welcome anyone who was interested in joining our open alumni network without requiring that they be graduates or have earned a certain number of credit hours. The conclusions we drew from our research told us not to create a closed, dues-paying membership society.

The Alumni Leadership Council meets quarterly over lunch. Other foundation staff members attend regularly, and I join the group occasionally. The college provides a modest annual budget of $30,000 to pay for alumni premiums and events, and the college marketing department produces all alumni communications as part of its budget. The foundation picks up incidental expenses.

I set the expectation early that Kirkwood's goal for the Alumni Leadership Council was not to raise funds, but instead to make friends and strengthen the alumni relationship with the college. The group adopted a mission statement focused on forming connections (among themselves and with the college) and began to create a schedule of events and communications vehicles. To gain visibility, they made occasional reports to both the foundation board and the college trustees.

Learner Success Agenda

In 2010, Kirkwood was ready for a new strategic plan. With the overall goal of increasing completion rates, we spent a full year developing our new plan, the Learner Success Agenda. The plan includes a number of strategic initiatives to strengthen Kirkwood. I knew it was important that the foundation and the alumni program have a strong connection to this plan, so both are integrated into our Regional Leadership initiative.

Kirkwood's tag line is "Start here, go anywhere!" It emphasizes the great start and wonderful possibilities that Kirkwood students have before them. I frequently use that tag line when I'm talking about the many paths our alumni travel.

Several years ago, one of Kirkwood's faculty members used ZIP codes of our alumni to create a map that shows where our former students live. The map illustrates both the strong alumni concentration in our local service region and the variety of far-flung places our alumni reach. Studying the map helps shape our marketing message, and it has given us some interesting ideas about where we might want to host a Kirkwood alumni event in the future.

Events and communications

Under Jody's guidance, the Alumni Leadership Council has developed into an active and cohesive group. Their ambitious approach has led to the creation of a busy events schedule that includes a strong alumni presence at dozens of existing college and community events, capped by a free-standing annual event, the Celebration of Success. This signature event is a formal awards dinner and alumni recognition event for 250 guests. With the foundation's involvement, it serves a strong donor cultivation and stewardship purpose as well. Sponsorship is coordinated carefully with foundation fundraising and keeps the cost of the ticket to $25.

Over the past several years, the communications outreach for both the alumni program and the foundation has grown and become more integrated. A newsletter for alumni and foundation donors, produced by our college marketing department, is mailed semiannually to all 70,000 alumni. An e-newsletter is sent monthly, and a social media strategy is in place.

In response to these pieces, we frequently receive emails from alumni who are pleased to hear news of Kirkwood and eager to share their stories. Recently a sales manager for a medical supply company wrote,

> "I fly into Cedar Rapids every so often as we work with a few consulting surgeons at the University of Iowa. And every time I land, I look towards the Kirkwood campus and smile to myself and think how far I've come from Cedar Rapids, Iowa to Naples, Florida. It's all about the opportunity and possibilities that Kirkwood brings to its students, and then what you do with it."

Recently, a number of academic departments have worked to enlist alumni who are professionals in specific areas to speak to their classes. Over the years, the Alumni Leadership Council has included increasingly prominent community members, and the group remains an active and engaged council of workers. Chris Wheeler, president of Point Builders in Cedar Rapids since 2010, is a proud member. "Kirkwood played an integral role in nurturing my leadership skills," he says. "I was glad to have a chance to get involved again as a member of the Alumni Leadership Council. Getting involved—that's the recipe for success."

Finding alumni

By 2011, after two years of consistent communication with Kirkwood alumni, we felt the time was right to launch an alumni donor acquisition program. RuffaloCODY, one of the nation's leading phonathon managers for educational fundraising (and recently rebranded as Ruffalo Noel Levitz), is a long-standing Kirkwood partner. The foundation staff had many discussions with the RuffaloCODY team about basing the Kirkwood calling script on information learned from the Epley research. The foundation committed to a three-year donor acquisition effort, with callers phoning all available alumni records. Each year the program broke even in terms of cost and pledges received, but due to pledge fulfillment rates of approximately 60 percent, it required an annual investment of about $15,000. The three-year program resulted in 1,500 new alumni donors who will now be segmented and solicited for renewed gifts as part of the foundation's annual appeal, and the foundation will work to identify high-potential prospects from this group.

As the alumni program has grown, the foundation has stepped up to support it behind the scenes. Kirkwood's operating agreement with the foundation is written to facilitate sharing of data so that, at the end of each semester, graduate records are transferred from the college system into the foundation database. The foundation regularly updates alumni mail and email addresses. To fully prepare to solicit alumni nationally, the foundation has completed registration for charitable solicitation (or confirmed exemption from registration) in all 50 states.

Real World Success campaign

The Kirkwood Foundation conducts a major fundraising campaign every five years, mainly to raise scholarship dollars. The Real World Success campaign was launched in May 2011, and the case statement and campaign video featured compelling stories about three Kirkwood alumni who had received scholarships, graduated and gone on to successful careers. The case statement also relied heavily on findings from our internal research showing that Kirkwood students who receive scholarships are more than twice as likely to graduate in three years as those who do not. This gave the campaign a firm connection both to our alumni program and to our completion agenda, the Learner Success Agenda.

The goal of the Real World Success campaign was $12.5 million. After just two years, we announced the successful conclusion of the campaign with nearly $19 million raised. The community received our requests warmly and supported us generously. I really believe the positive buzz of 70,000 engaged alumni helped create the culture for our fundraising to succeed.

Purple Heart Scholarship

In fall 2013, an anonymous donor gave the foundation $350,000 to create a Purple Heart Scholarship for recipients of the military honor, their spouses or children. The husband and wife behind the gift are Kirkwood alumni. They were nontraditional students balancing family life with full-time jobs and college courses. In a news release, the couple praised Kirkwood for being "a great school for working parents."

"Quality education that is conveniently available is hard to come by," one of the donors said in a statement. "Given the affordable cost and the high caliber of education I received, I think Kirkwood is an outstanding value." The Purple Heart Scholarship will cover the cost of tuition and books for recipients for their entire two-year stay at Kirkwood.

What a great example of an alumni gift! Although it wasn't specifically solicited, it followed several years of alumni outreach that I believe helped make it possible. As the visibility of alumni giving to Kirkwood grows, I believe there will be more gifts like this in the future.

Evaluation

I know many community colleges have struggled with how to evaluate their alumni programs. I often say that Kirkwood is "the community's college," and the enthusiasm and engagement of our alumni is a key factor in our place in the community. In the past five years, during a time when both city and K–12 votes in our area failed, Kirkwood passed two bond and levy votes with record high percentages of voter approval. Our largest fundraising campaign ever exceeded its goal by 50 percent, and our media coverage is extensive and overwhelmingly positive. Although none of that can be attributed directly to our alumni program, I'd like to think the consistent alumni outreach and engagement efforts have had a hand in those successes.

One of the best ways to show the alumni program's value is to match its activities back to the college's Learner Success Agenda. For example, our alumni help with our strategic goal of creating community liaisons to expand Kirkwood's regional relationships. Our strategic goal of creating a graduate follow-up survey has a natural alumni link.

As a former math teacher, I like metrics. But I understand that the heart of development work is about building relationships, and not everything can be quantified. I support the alumni program for the same reason I support Kirkwood's planned giving program: It helps build and maintain relationships that will pay off for Kirkwood over the long haul.

Steps to success

If you don't have an alumni program at your community college, or if you need to reinvigorate a lagging program, here are a few steps to get started:

- Talk to your foundation, make sure they're on board and find the right staff champion.
- Build an internal, cross-departmental team to think about the program, its value and its goals. The alumni program may be housed in the foundation, but it needs to be embraced by the whole college to be successful.
- Survey your alumni to learn about the relationships they have with your college and what kind of connections they would like to have. Base your plans on what you learn.
- Take care of the necessary initial housekeeping. Define "alumni" for your institution, and share alumni records with the foundation.
- Form an external alumni leadership group, and set the expectation for the group's purpose.
- Work with the leadership group to determine a communications and events plan. Implement in stages as resources allow.
- Consider an alumni donor acquisition effort (phonathon or direct mail).
- Celebrate your successes!

Looking ahead

As I reflect on the growth of Kirkwood's alumni program over the past five years, I'm pleased with how far we've come. We've systematized methods of communicating with our alumni and created events that are now eagerly anticipated annual gatherings. We've begun to integrate alumni giving into our annual appeals, and we're taking advantage of alumni connections to boost enrollment and recruitment efforts. Most important, the program has raised the profile of thousands of Kirkwood alumni who live in our community, and it helps everyone in this area to realize that Kirkwood really is "the community's college."

It's exciting to think of the possibilities ahead. The Kirkwood Foundation's planned giving program is a good example of an early investment that, with time, has paid off many times over. I believe Kirkwood's support of the Alumni & Friends program will bring that same benefit in the future, showing us again that relationships are the key to our growth.

Chapter 16

GETTING REAL, VIRTUALLY

The Tangible Benefits of a Social Media Persona

By @LeeLambert3

My name is Lee D. Lambert. I am chancellor of Pima Community College. And I tweet.

I tweet to inspire:

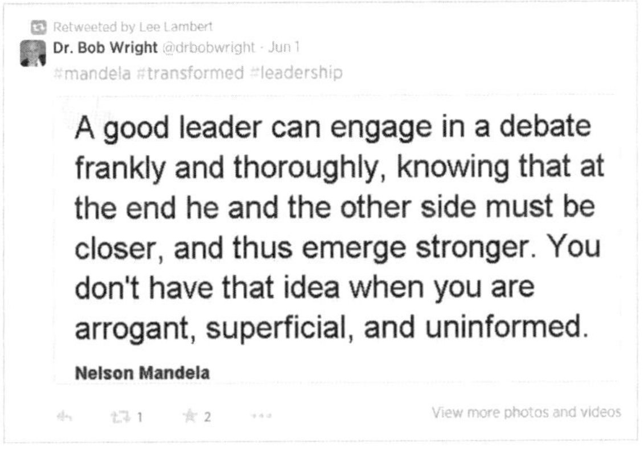

I tweet to promote the achievements of the students of Pima Community College (PCC), a multicampus district whose programs and services help some 50,000 residents of Tucson, Arizona, achieve their academic and professional goals in pursuit of their personal vision of the American Dream:

And I tweet to ... well, did you *see* the 2014 Super Bowl? (The less said about the 2015 Super Bowl, the better.)

So I tweet to celebrate. Not incidentally, I am a longtime resident of the Seattle area who came to PCC from Shoreline Community College in July 2013.

I also blog, offering 300- to 500-word posts a few times a week on a variety of topics of interest to external as well as internal audiences. Typical posts include a recounting of a Q & A session at a staff development event; an explanation of the impact of our strategic planning process, along with a call for public involvement; and the coming nationwide community college leadership exodus. (I should disclose up front that my blogs often discuss the college's response to probation. PCC received that sanction from its accreditor, the Higher Learning Commission, in April 2013, three months before I began working at the college. In December 2014 an evaluation team recommended that the college be removed from probation. We expect by March 2015 to have regained the fullest confidence of the Higher Learning Commission.)

In sum, I have a fairly well-rounded social media persona. And I hold that in the 21st century, community college leaders must be engaged on social media in order to further the mission of their institutions. Specifically, any CEO who is not reaching out via social media is missing an opportunity to support his or her school's development efforts. The historical three-part mission of higher education development—communication, philanthropy and alumni relations—can be advanced in a small yet potentially significant way by the strategic deployment of the CEO's "voice" in the digital realm.

Time can be money

Community college leaders realize very quickly that the most precious commodity in their world is time. As chancellor, I am committed to connecting in the most profound way with students, faculty and staff, as well as with potential partners in business, education, government and the community. In my first year at PCC, I have met with close to 2,000 people, yet I know there are thousands more with whom I should connect. I am acutely aware of this paradox of our times: As the virtual world has crept into so many lives, real human engagement—two people talking to each other—becomes even more important in determining how well community college thought leaders and decision makers lead their organizations.

For those charged with advancement, the problem is that the people they need to reach are numerous, diverse and can live hundreds or thousands of miles away. And asking for support is especially challenging in these still-precarious economic times. But social media can help, by introducing the college, through its leaders, in an informal way that strangely seems more personal despite the fact that it is occurring virtually. Every organization needs to speak to its potential donors. Social media is a particularly efficient means of introducing the organization to those donors. Through posts, tweets, blogs and photos, you can use your laptop or smartphone to interact with countless individuals. The subtle goal is to make them seem more comfortable supporting the community college because they feel they know you and can trust you—even before they've actually met you. It's kind of like online dating. You are casting a wide net and putting forward your best online face in the hope of finding those who, eventually, will fall for your organization in a tangible way.

Lessons from Shoreline

I served as president of Shoreline Community College, near Seattle, from 2007 to 2013. Following a 2009 American Council on Education conference that included sessions on social media, I realized that community college leaders, in order to help shape the voice of their institutions, had a responsibility to become involved. At the time, Shoreline had no social media presence, and I knew this was no time to maintain the status quo. The rationale for the initiative was obvious: to articulate the institution's vision, to broaden its reach and to show that the institution was open to engagement in order to attract investment.

The payoff was tangible. Shoreline was able to leverage that virtual foray into the community with advocacy and information-sharing at a person-to-person level, resulting in collaborations that brought resources from area industry into the college and helped Shoreline further its mission.

There are several lessons here: Often, Shoreline was engaged by its area partners not through its foundation but through those college leaders with whom they had interfaced previously; anyone can be a point of contact for opportunities. Moreover, when deciding to engage on social media, I had to determine the boundaries for disclosing personal information, a decision that CEOs will have to decide for themselves.

The benefits of friends

A small but growing body of research suggests that social media can level the philanthropic playing field and enable smaller organizations to compete with larger groups for donors. Take, for example, the 2014 study "The Social Network Effect: Determinants of Giving Through Social Media," by Gregory Saxton, associate professor in the University at Buffalo Department of Communication, and Lili Wang, assistant professor of nonprofit studies in the Arizona State University School of Community Resources and Development.

According to a May 2014 article on scienceblog.com, the study analyzed the fundraising activities of more than 50 organizations using Facebook for that purpose. Donors on social media sites do not seem to care how large an organization is, the researchers say. Instead, they are influenced by the "social network effect," which is sparked by the size of an organization's network of followers. In short, an organization with a lot of online friends has a better chance of receiving donations.

This study and other research contending that social media can not only raise the online profile of even small organizations, but also increase their support bases and their ability to generate donations online and offline, has not escaped notice at our college. PCC coexists peaceably yet competitively in Tucson with our academic partner, the University of Arizona, a learning institution of global renown with hundreds of thousands of former Wildcat alumni and a multibillion-dollar budget that includes line items covering an impressive array of resources dedicated to development. PCC is exploring an expansion of the social media presence of the PCC Foundation (our development arm) and the alumni association. We know we need an edge, and your community college likely needs one, too.

Building an effective framework

A few words are in order on the necessity of having the proper organizational structure in place. From a CEO's perspective, it is necessary to create a structure that clusters functions so that they work effectively and efficiently. Whatever organizational walls exist between advancement, public relations, marketing (both online and offline) and IT must be torn down, for reasons that should be clear to you instinctively and will become even clearer, I hope, later in the chapter. Similarly, other related functions—everything from event planning to enrollment management to external/community relations—should be brought out of the silos that hinder their effectiveness and gathered under a single umbrella. At the time of this writing, PCC is engaged in an organizational redesign that will charge an executive administrator with the task of integrating the aforementioned areas into a cohesive working unit.

Writing: A checklist

Assuming that your college's organizational house is in order, you, as CEO, are charged with writing. Having associated with community college presidents for two decades, I know (a) they occasionally need help in this area and (b) they are fond of checklists. So, here are some things to consider as you sit down before the keyboard:

- **Audience and purpose.** Typically, the audience for any community college leader's communications is a wide variety of internal and external constituencies. (Nowadays, anyone on Earth with an Internet connection is a potential reader, donor, business partner or vociferous and rabid critic, so remember to choose your words with particular care.) But your primary audience comprises folks who might be predisposed to furthering the college's advancement efforts, such as alumni, or engaging with the college in a tangible, fruitful way, such as "C-suite" decision makers in business, government, education and community- and faith-based organizations; in other words, they are people who might bestow valuable resources on the college.
- **Voice.** Your audience wants to hear from *you*; you are the chief marketing officer for the college in this arena. You are making a foray into social media in order to establish a personal connection with the aforementioned decision makers. This could be an issue if you don't have a personality. Leaders of institutions of higher learning are often perceived, rightly or wrongly, as aloof, distant dignitaries who tend toward verbosity and rarely stray from an institutional voice. You will need to fight any impulse toward imperiousness. Instead of prefacing a sentence with "It is the considered opinion of the college..." substitute "I believe ... ." Be brief: Don't use seven words when two will do. You will need to write from the heart, not from the position paper. In short, you will need to sound like a human being conversing with another human being—the gold standard of communication.

- **Medium.** I blog and tweet because they are the formats best suited to my personality, writing style and needs as a CEO. Tweets allow me to get my points across in 140-character bursts. Their necessary brevity means I can touch on a variety of often controversial issues simply by linking to articles in the media, or by retweeting. Moreover, I can display my personal side efficiently without oversharing or devoting an inordinate amount of effort. (Tweeting about the Seahawks is appropriate; sitting down and writing a 500-word blog about them might be perceived as an odd use of a CEO's valuable time—not that I couldn't. But I digress.)

  Blogs are an effective way to quickly tell the story of the college and to address topics that may come up in the media. They are a good substitute for antiquated weekly "Chancellor's Reports." In today's 24/7 world, an issue raised in the morning must be tackled that afternoon. The underlying, positive message to your readers (and potential partners) in the community is that the institution listens, is responsive, is on top of the situation and just may be worth doing business with in the future.
- **Content.** Content is king. There is no substitute for substance and honesty. Remember Mark Twain's aphorism, "When in doubt tell the truth." Trumpet your institution's successes with full-throated enthusiasm. However, if your college has screwed up, admit the error, clearly explain how it happened and detail your plan for fixing the problem. Do not spin. Your audiences, particularly your younger audiences, are hypersensitive to being marketed to.
- **Responsibilities.** Avoid the hard sell; that's what your development team is for. Keep the conversation going. If you occasionally don't have time to blog, tweet or post to Facebook, delegate responsibility to qualified staff. If someone comments or asks a question of you on social media, respond. If someone follows you on Twitter, follow him or her back. The worst mistake you can make is to appear unheeding or inattentive. Silence is lethal.

An integrated effort

In *The Tipping Point*, author Malcolm Gladwell identifies people he terms "connectors" as essential to organizational achievement. Connectors link individuals and organizations for mutual benefit. At PCC, I have made it a priority for campus presidents and vice presidents, along with top-level executives in academics, IT, finance and human resources to be the college's connectors, engaging their counterparts in the community on social media as well as, of course, face-to-face. Through blogs and message boards, these executives discuss issues of mutual interest with their counterparts outside of higher education. They help demystify the world of higher education administration, which can appear opaque and nebulous to the unfamiliar. They offer an entry point to the college.

Just because you blog it, don't assume it will be read. We are competing for the attention of an audience inundated with opportunities to engage on the Internet. That is why my blogs and those of my team are part of a weekly PCC Foundation e-newsletter that is pushed out to the 26,000-plus members of the PCC Alumni Association, as well as to 1,500 community leaders, via an email blast. We view these newsletters as a way to engage the community, to tell the story of the college free of the filter of the media. Our social media messages are going to those constituents who have had a positive experience at PCC—graduates—in order to further development and engagement.

In conclusion: Of values and hashtags

In the mid-2000s, a local man in the final stages of his life received exemplary care at the hands of nurses and technicians who had learned their craft at Pima Community College. He instructed his descendants to engage PCC development officials, resulting in a $1 million donation to the PCC Foundation. It remains the largest single donation the college has received in its nearly 50-year history. The gift has allowed the college to advance the educational opportunities of hundreds of students in countless ways.

Social media played no role in the bequest. At the time, Twitter was merely a notion, and Facebook wasn't the global behemoth it is today. The keys were our graduates; they were the "connectors," to use Gladwell's parlance, who, through their expertise and character, served as the best ambassadors a community college can have. I note this to highlight the ultimate determinants in the success of any development initiative and, really, any endeavor your organization seeks to undertake: your values (those of your leadership and of your college as a whole) and your college's effectiveness in making measurable advances toward fulfilling its mission.

As I said earlier, PCC has been on probation for the failure of previous leadership to comply with our accreditor's standards regarding governance and administration. While under the sanction, donations to the college, not surprisingly, suffered. We are well on our way to getting our house in order, and I am confident that our advancement efforts will bear more fruit. But until we have regained the fullest confidence of our accreditor and the community, all the hashtags and search engine optimization and Instagram-ing in the world won't make a difference in advancement or any other arena. Social media is not a panacea. It's a tool—an arrow in a quiver. It can hit its mark only if the institution is healthy and vibrant. Community colleges must be committed to student success, aligning with the needs of their diverse communities, and maintaining access and affordability. Only when you, as CEO, have fulfilled those commitments will it make sense to engage on social media for purposes of development. Only then will you have a great story to tell.

Paul Schwalbach, public information manager at Pima Community College, contributed to this chapter.

Chapter 17

WHEN—NOT IF—A CRISIS HITS YOUR CAMPUS

By John J. "Ski" Sygielski and Linnie S. Carter

Crises in higher education are inevitable. Whether the crisis is related to a crime on campus or a sex scandal, community college presidents and their executive teams have to know how to effectively manage and communicate about them. In this chapter, you will learn how a new community college president and the college's crisis team managed multiple crises, including a student abduction, an accreditation warning and an embezzlement.

HACC, Central Pennsylvania's Community College, is the largest and oldest community college in Pennsylvania. With more than 20,000 students and five campuses, the college has a strong legacy, reputation and brand. I (John J. "Ski" Sygielski) was hired as president in July 2011, and I (Linnie S. Carter) joined the college as the vice president of college advancement in March 2012. Fortunately, we had experience that helped us effectively lead when the college experienced six major crises in a short period of time.

How the crises unfolded

The following crises occurred within a seven-month period, beginning in fall 2012:

- **Accreditation warning.** In November 2012 the college learned from its accrediting body that it would be on warning if several criteria were not met. The possible impact was probation and suspension of accreditation.
- **Student abduction.** A female student was abducted from a campus in December 2012, which traumatized and devastated the college community.

- **Embezzlement.** Also in December 2012, it was revealed that a former vice president at the college was being investigated for possible misuse of college funds. The potential impact was enormous: loss of public support and increased scrutiny from the public and government agencies.
- **Bond rating decrease.** Standard and Poor's lowered the college's long-term rating to A– from A in February 2013. A possible consequence was a loss of confidence in the college's fiscal management.
- **Layoffs.** For the first time in many years, the college had a significant number of layoffs due to budgetary challenges. In May 2013 the college eliminated filled and unfilled positions. This resulted in a decrease in morale and, in some cases, the loss of high performers.
- **Lawsuit.** An employee filed a federal lawsuit against the college in June 2013. A possible impact was a loss of trust in the college administration.

What we did; what you'll need

Fortunately, we had most of the elements of our crisis plan in place when these events began unfolding. This preparation enabled us to respond quickly and confidently, and helped minimize damage to our reputation.

A crisis plan should include the following elements:

- A clearly defined crisis management team
- Crisis management logistics plan
- Crisis communications plan
- Tools to help manage crises

The president, executive team, public relations and marketing team, and safety and security staff should meet quarterly to review and practice the crisis management plans. The governing board should review the plans annually.

You should have multiple copies of the plans—one in your office, one at your home, one in your work bag and one you can access electronically. In the event of a crisis, you should be able to access the plans within seconds—even if there is no electricity or computer access. Keep an electronic copy on a flash drive along with the print versions to expedite communications.

Crisis management team

A clear structure with decision-making responsibilities should be outlined—and it probably will not mirror your organizational chart. Keep the core team manageable in size, and include others only when necessary. At a minimum, your team should include the following members:

- **The president.** The leader of the college needs to be involved in all aspects of the crisis, since he or she will be held accountable for how the event is handled.

- **The president's executive team.** They must leverage and marshal the talents of the teams they lead and thus need to be well versed about the crisis as well.
- **The head of public relations and marketing.** This person's team will be on the front lines communicating about the crisis and thus needs to know everything—the good, the bad and the ugly.
- **The head of safety and security.** This person most often will lead the execution of the crisis management logistics plan.

Since crises can occur at any time, you should have at least one—and preferably two—backup people identified for key positions on the team.

Crisis management logistics plan

Developing a crisis management logistics plan should be a team commitment and top-priority project. All of the crisis management team members should be part of the plan development, and they should be actively engaged in the process to vet and finalize the plan.

Crisis management logistic plans should include the following components:

- The **table of contents** will allow you to briefly navigate the plan in the event of a crisis.
- The **executive summary** briefly describes the purpose, format and use of the plan.
- **Contact information** for the entire college crisis management team will allow you to contact them quickly. The contact information should include professional and personal contact information, including telephone numbers and email addresses.
- A designated **incident command center**—with alternate locations—where your team can meet. The centers should include ample phone lines, computers and a fax machine. Two-way radios and bullhorns should be available there or through safety and security.
- You will also need **contact information for the law enforcement agencies** located in your college's service area. The main points of contacts include police chiefs, sheriffs and district attorneys.
- You will need to use a **variety of strategies** for handling crises—especially those that threaten the safety and security of students, employees and visitors. The plan should include information about how to handle crises ranging from power outages and severe weather to a shooter on campus or a bomb threat.
- Include **floor plans** of the buildings on your campuses. This is crucial for colleges with multiple campuses or buildings. You will also need a list of **off-site venues** to which you can relocate in the event of a major crisis that may result in injuries or the loss of life (for example, a natural disaster, a shooting or a hostage situation).

Crisis communications plan

The most common criticism colleges receive during and after crises relates to communication. Communication can be one of the most challenging aspects of any situation, as it is virtually impossible to communicate quickly or frequently enough.

Be ready with a communications plan that includes the following elements:

- The **table of contents** will allow you to briefly and quickly navigate the plan.
- The **executive summary** briefly describes the purpose, format and use of the crisis communications plan.
- **Contact information** for the entire college crisis management team. This should include professional and personal contact information, including telephone numbers and email addresses.
- **Contact information for the public information officers of law enforcement agencies** located in your college's service area. In the event of a crisis, the college crisis communications team will need to coordinate with their public information officers.
- **Media contact information,** including home or cell numbers, if possible, since you may not have immediate access to email.
- Contact information for **key constituents and influencers,** especially those whom you may need to advocate for the college. This includes your board of trustees, foundation board and the head of your faculty council or unions—even key local officials such as the mayor, city manager or head of the Chamber of Commerce.
- **Pre-written content** about a variety of crises, so that it can be quickly copied and pasted onto websites, into news releases, onto social media and into email messages.
- You will need to use a **variety of tactics** to communicate with your internal and external stakeholders. (Internal stakeholders include students, employees and board members. External stakeholders include alumni, donors, media outlets and the general population.) You should include a list of these tactics in the plan. Examples include news releases, email messages, social media sites, websites, news releases, blogs, conference calls, town hall meetings and forums. If **usernames and passwords** are needed to access the tactics, include this information in the plan.
- Include a **checklist** that covers the immediate, short-term and long-term steps to communicate about the crisis. This checklist may save lives, so be sure it is comprehensive and easy to use. It should be formatted into five columns: step (or task) number, task (begins with a verb), person responsible, deadline (for example, immediately, within 12 hours and within 24 hours) and status (for example, done and not applicable).

Developing key messages

To communicate effectively during a crisis, you have to know your stakeholders well, empathize with them, communicate openly with them, listen to them often and use common sense. If you do, you will be able to develop effective key messages that will resonate with most of your target audiences.

An institution of higher education that experiences a **student abduction** might have these key messages:

- An abduction has been reported at the college.
- The victim has been located and is receiving medical care. However, please stay alert and take normal precautions.

- We are reviewing procedures to determine how we can make our campus safer and will keep you informed of enhancements.

Due to the severity and nature of this type of crisis, you would use an alert system and partner with local law enforcement agencies. You should communicate with all internal and external stakeholders—as often as necessary—to prevent panic from ensuing. You should then provide regular updates on how your organization is beefing up your safety and security procedures. Also, it would be important for you to monitor social media, email and comments that are posted on online articles, because an abduction will definitely attract significant media coverage.

Suppose your organization is plagued by an alleged **embezzlement** by a high-level official. Your key messages might be the following:

- We are cooperating fully with the district attorney's office.
- We will defer further comment pending conclusion of the investigation.
- The accused's employment has been terminated.
- We have reviewed and modified our processes, procedures and systems to help ensure these types of situations do not occur in the future.

These types of crises will require that your legal team and human resources team are actively engaged in the management and communication of the crisis.

Communicate about the embezzlement once you have been cleared to do so by your legal, human resources and public relations teams. These teams may have different opinions about how to communicate about the crisis, so do what is in the best interest of your organization. Avoid using legal reasons for not providing information. Be as transparent and open as possible while remaining mindful of privacy issues.

Monitoring your communication channels—including email messages, social media sites and comments online—will help you to determine how effective your key messaging is, how it needs to be modified and how often it needs to be communicated.

Finally, **employee layoffs** might be considered a crisis for your organization—especially if they do not occur often.

Your key messages might include these:

- The college has painstakingly adopted a balanced budget.
- Unfortunately, to do so, we must eliminate filled and unfilled positions.
- Those colleagues whose positions are being eliminated will be treated fairly, professionally and humanely. They will receive severance packages and assistance with finding new jobs.
- Change is difficult but necessary to remain fiscally sound and competitive in today's economy.

This type of crisis will be emotionally charged, since it will result in people losing their livelihoods. Employees not being laid off will feel guilty and possibly resentful toward the leadership team. With this particular crisis, you must communicate with your internal audiences early, often and openly. The primary method of communication with employees might be email, forums and town hall meetings. Also, to allow employees to voice their opinions anonymously, set up an online form that does not require them to disclose their identity. Address these anonymous concerns to all employees—via email, your newsletter and in forums or town hall meetings. Social media may not be an appropriate communications tool for this type of feedback from employees.

Tools to help manage crises

Many economical tools can be used to help manage and communicate about crises. Here are some of the commonly used ones:

TYPES OF TOOLS	POSSIBLE USES
Conference calls	Conference calls are needed for the crisis management team to provide and receive updates and to communicate with other stakeholders, including board members and the media. Be sure the access information is confidential and shared with a limited number of people. This approach will help ensure that unauthorized individuals are not listening in on your conference calls.
Email messages	Have email distribution lists already established for your stakeholder groups, including the crisis management team, board members, employees and media outlets. During a crisis, you will not have time to create these email lists. Create them today to ensure you will be ready in the event of a crisis. If your email system cannot handle large numbers of email addresses, consider investing in a system that allows you to do email blasts to large numbers of people. An example of such a system is Vertical Response.
Social media	Use social media sites to communicate during crises. The most effective ones are Facebook and Twitter. Make sure the sites appropriately represent your organization and include the logo. Include the username and password of the sites in the crisis communications plan.

Newsletters	Once the crisis dies down, address it in your organization's newsletter—whether the newsletter is distributed by mail or email. Do not pretend the crisis never happened. Your stakeholders will lose trust in you if you do.
Website	Make sure you have a bare-bones home page of your website ready to go live on a moment's notice, so that you can provide frequent updates and links to resources, depending on the situation (counselors, for example). The last thing you want during a disaster is a home page with your traditional photos of happy, smiling students and employees. You also want to quickly establish the website as a credible, timely place to get information.
Forums and town hall meetings	Communicate about the crisis with your major stakeholders in person. Forums and town hall meetings are quite effective. Work with the crisis management team to develop the agenda, determine who will speak, outline the key messages and anticipate questions that may be asked. These materials can be used for news conferences if you feel news conferences are appropriate when communicating about the crisis. If the forums and town hall meetings need to occur online, tools like Adobe Connect are very effective.
Videos	Videography is important when communicating about crises—especially major ones. Determine the best person to speak on behalf the organization (typically the president), develop a script and practice it with the speaker and quickly produce and distribute the video. Your organization should have a YouTube channel, so the video should definitely be posted there.
Alert systems	Alert systems are particularly effective with colleges and allow them to communicate with students and employees—via text message and/or email—very quickly. Colleges with large numbers of stakeholders and those that have multiple campuses and buildings should invest in an alert system. Doing so could save lives.

Guiding principles for managing crises

When managing crises, it is important to remember and adhere to the following guiding principles:

- **"Family" comes first.** Your internal stakeholders should hear about the crisis first. And they definitely should hear about the crisis before the media inform them.
- **Tell your own story.** Do not hesitate to share information about the crisis. Disclosing the crisis yourself allows you to better control the crisis and messaging, and it builds credibility.
- **Be ready for anything.** Prepare for anything—no matter how big or small the situation is. Being blindsided worsens a crisis, so be vigilant and stay ready.
- **Know that nothing is a secret.** Confidentiality and discretion are not as valued today as they once were. Remember that nothing is a secret, and information may be leaked—even by those you thought you could trust. Therefore, be savvy and smart—and even a little cautious—when communicating intimate details about the crisis.
- **Be available 24/7.** Crises are not planned; they have a life of their own. When they occur, organizations need to adopt an all-hands-on-deck philosophy and mentality. All members of the crisis management team must be available every day, all day—for as long as necessary—to ensure the crisis is managed and communicated about effectively.
- **Protect your emotional, physical and spiritual health.** No matter how much professional experience you have and how strong you are, managing crises is stressful and difficult. The president has to be the voice of reason and a pillar of strength during crises. However, when not in the public eye, the president needs to have an outlet and the listening ear of someone he or she can trust implicitly. Presidents are not superheroes—they are mere mortals. Therefore, protect your emotional, physical and spiritual health. You will be no good to anyone if you do not make your health a top priority. Find healthy strategies to vent and release the stress. A supportive significant other, a close friend, a good book or movie, exercise, a vacation—these are all viable options for recalibrating after managing a crisis.

Lessons learned

Let's fast forward to 2015 to see how these crises are being resolved:

- **Accreditation warning.** The warning was lifted in June 2014.
- **Student abduction.** No major crimes have occurred on a campus since December 2012.
- **Embezzlement.** The former vice president was sentenced to 15 months in prison.
- **Bond rating decrease.** The college's bond rating is holding steady.
- **Layoffs.** There have been no significant layoffs since May 2013.
- **Lawsuit.** The federal lawsuit is still pending.

We learned some important lessons along the way:

- **Accreditation warning.** Maintain regular focus and review to ensure academic programs, services and initiatives are in adherence with accreditation standards.
- **Student abduction.** Develop and maintain professional relationships with local law enforcement agencies.
- **Embezzlement.** Ensure appropriate checks and balances and systems are in place to keep employees honest.
- **Bond rating decrease.** Communicate often with the bonding agency to ensure its understanding of changes occurring with the college (for example, enrollment and accreditation).
- **Layoffs.** Provide information on layoffs and other organizational changes to the internal college community before providing that information to the external community, including the media.
- **Lawsuit.** Ensure the college has an effective working relationship with local media outlets.
- **All crises.** Develop strong alliances during the good times so that they can be leveraged during the bad times.

Assessment of your crisis management logistics plan and crisis communications plan is critical. To determine how effective they are and how well your stakeholders are bouncing back from a crisis, survey them, conduct focus groups and invite them to forums and town hall meetings. Use the research to improve your processes and plans. Be thick skinned and grateful for the opportunity to engage with your stakeholders. Their involvement is a good thing. It means they care. As we know, that is half the battle.

Chapter 18

MARKETING FROM THE INSIDE OUT

By Robert L. Breuder

Is there anyone who doesn't know Coca-Cola, McDonald's or Verizon? These companies already have sales in the billions each year, yet they are the first to drop millions for a minute-long advertisement during the Super Bowl. The leaders of these companies, who live or die by their profit margins, know the value of marketing.

I am heading into my 34th year as a community college president. Over the years it has become only more evident to me that consistent marketing is a necessity if you want to build a sustainable institution. It is not something to be indulged in when times are good, only to be jettisoned during the lean years as a way to cut costs. Nor should marketing be simply punted to the marketing department. In truth, it is the sum total effort of every employee on your campus. You as a president must actively take part in marketing your institution. Your administrators, faculty and staff will follow your lead.

Marketing is not just a billboard or an ad or an advertorial in your newspaper's educational section. Marketing is your way to *tell your institution's story*—to share your value with prospective students and the community. It's a way to encase the mission, initiatives and outcomes that define your organization.

I've led three different community colleges over nearly 34 years. When I first arrived on each campus, I found weaknesses in the products on their shelves, physical plants and financials—all key components to our ability to market. I hope that some of the lessons learned and examples I share here make their way into your own thinking as you decide how best to promote your institution. Some educators shy away from referring to their college as a business or from using business terms to describe what they do, but I do not. I am a strong proponent of the Five Ps: People, Product, Price, Place and Promotion. I have placed promotion last on this list—not because it is the least important but because, without the first four, no amount of promotion will be effective.

People: Every employee is a marketer

People are your foundation. You must have skilled individuals in place to achieve your marketing and communication goals. Or, as I like to say, you must have the "right person in the right box." If you do not have the right person leading your promotional activity, you need to face some difficult decisions immediately. When I arrived at each of the three colleges where I served as president (Pennsylvania College of Technology, in Williamsport, Penn.; Harper College, in Palatine, Ill.; and College of DuPage, in Glen Ellyn, Ill.), one of my first actions was to hire an experienced marketing leader and team.

As in any other business, you must be willing to spend money on marketing to make money and to increase awareness and improve the perception of your institution. My experience says to spend between 2 and 4 percent of your operating budget on marketing, but there isn't a one-size-fits-all answer to how much you should invest—and continue to invest. It will depend on your college's size and enrollment goals. But if you want to get ahead, you have to give marketing the resources, which means providing your team the necessary budget, space and staffing. Don't be surprised if when asked for a frank response, your marketing person says you need to up your budget. It's been my experience that community college leaders generally suffer from a mentality of not believing they have to make a real investment in marketing; they assume that just turning on the lights is enough. The same is true of staffing. Does your shop have the people in place to accomplish what you want to do? Do you have the expertise in house to handle graphics, writing, project management, and the like? Is your facility small enough (or large enough) to warrant outsourcing a percentage of your work?

Having an effective marketing team is only the first step. Next, recognize that each and every employee at your college is an essential marketer. Employees must be informed and have the resources needed to successfully tell your story. And they must internalize their role in customer relations. College of DuPage maintains a customer service training program for all employees. Most people learn through repetition, and I have found that after a message is communicated three times, it resonates and is absorbed.

At College of DuPage, I pen a Monday internal e-newsletter that includes information about happenings at the college as well as larger, more issues-based pieces concerning higher education regionally and nationally. This past year, we had 36,000 unique opens for this online publication and an average "read time" of more than 8.5 minutes per person. In addition, we have a lighter Friday newsletter, the *Green Sheet*, which is picture heavy and focuses largely on college, faculty and student successes. However, important information that must be understood and become the "language" of our employees will show up in the *Green Sheet* as well. These internal newsletters can be very effective if you take the time to ensure good, interesting, pertinent content. I recently used my Monday newsletter to correct statements made about the college by an outside tax watchdog group. I was gratified to receive several positive comments from employees who read my clarifications, including this one: "I felt a sense of pride when I read it. Very informative. I knew what was being said in the papers probably wasn't true, but it was good to see it on paper. And the President's pride in this place and his employees really came through."

We host monthly managerial meetings during which information is dispersed and discussed—and then passed on to direct reports—so that our employees are empowered with messages and news they can share with their neighbors, family and friends outside the college. College leadership also meets with classified staff leadership quarterly, our faculty communication committee and the college's Shared Governance Council.

Word of mouth is vital to the strength of an institution. We understand this at College of DuPage and view our students as important ambassadors for the college. I personally host regular "Pizza with the President" sessions to answer students' questions and let them know about issues affecting the college. In addition, we have a student trustee on our board, student ambassadors who represent our college at multiple events and activities, and strong relationships with the editors of the student newspaper, which serves as an effective messaging vehicle among students as well as staff members on campus. I also meet with student leaders on the same day as our monthly board of trustees meetings. You must equip each and every employee and student with the resources they need to feel comfortable *and driven* to spread the word about your institution. I personally have made a point to visit multiple college offices for three hours at a time to learn how I can better market all aspects of the college.

Product: Adapt and change, then do it again

Students and their parents have more choices than ever when it comes to higher education. To compete, community colleges, like any business, need to produce what consumers want and make it easy for those consumers to work with them. Think of your college as a business. You must have the right products on the shelves for your customers (students) to buy your merchandise (academic programs). To do this, your academic affairs department, faculty members and administrators must be aware of the needs of students and the area workforce. Flexibility and the willingness to adapt programming are key components of success. (I feel this is an area in which community colleges can move more nimbly than our four-year counterparts.) At College of DuPage, we elicit this information from a wide range of "listening posts," including advisory boards comprised of regional business leaders, which report to our academic divisions. In addition, our administrators get out from behind their desks and visit with area organizations such as chambers of commerce, Rotary clubs and high school counselors and advisors to learn what students need and what the marketplace is dictating. We also host multiple "Community Nights" each year at the college to gather input from area business, educational and government leaders; we then feed this information into our five-year strategic plan. Twice-yearly meetings with residents living adjacent to the college offer additional opportunities to share information and address interests.

I can't stress enough the importance of staying on top of career and programming trends. You and your team must always be looking around the corner for the next innovation. Over the past five years at College of DuPage, we have added more than 60 new certificate and degree programs. Most recently, we have added an advanced certificate in proton therapy, a music business degree, a certificate in perioperative nursing, and a culinology and food science degree. These offerings are varied, but each one stems from listening to our constituents and creating programs from this input that ultimately offer students solid career opportunities. On the flip side, difficult decisions must be made regarding programs that have become out of date or for other reasons are not filling classrooms. They must be removed from the shelf and replaced with merchandise (programming) in tune with the market of today and, more important, tomorrow. You should be prepared for resistance from those who have a vested interest in a particular program.

We listen to our students. As a result, we now offer specialized programming in the form of study abroad, online courses and online certificate/degree programs, service learning, and an innovative 3+1 program that enables students to earn 12 different baccalaureate degrees from partnering universities entirely on our campus at a significantly reduced tuition rate. I am currently leading a statewide effort to change state statute so that community colleges in Illinois can offer specialized baccalaureate degrees. Countless times in my conversations with students and through information gleaned from faculty and administrators, we have heard about the unmet need to offer baccalaureate degrees, especially in the areas of technology, manufacturing and health care. We have the people, curriculum, accreditation and facilities in place to offer these programs. It's really a no-brainer, but we know it will be a time-consuming proposition to bring this change to fruition. Regardless of the difficulty of the process, as a leader, you must be willing to think *and step* outside the box to offer new opportunities in education. In doing so, you call attention to your college as a place of innovation and excellence. Tell your story.

As I will discuss later under "Price," you must highlight the quality of your product if you are to counteract uninformed biases against attending a community college (whether we're willing to say it or not, much of the marketing we do is to counteract the stigma sometimes associated with community colleges, that we are somehow less than our four-year peers). How others see us begins with how we view ourselves.

I mentioned earlier the ease with which people should be able to access your products. I suggest you take an unflinching look at your institution's website. If feedback indicates a need, consider investing in the redesign of your site to ensure seamless customer interaction. Also take a look at how easily people can access your services in person. At College of DuPage we created Campus Central, a physical location in the midst of student services where visitors can have any question answered about where they need to go on campus. We want to make it as easy as possible for our students.

Price: Return on investments extend beyond Wall Street

Price and accessibility are traditionally strengths for community colleges when compared to four-year or for-profit institutions. We also offer and publicize many scholarships and programs meant to keep down the price even more. However, I believe you must be careful when touting your low price. The average member of the public might not know that most community colleges are supported significantly through tax dollars and assume that the low price means cheap and of low value, rather than affordable. Whether in your own public comments or in your advertising, you must counterbalance your message of price with quality and return on investment. For example, our students who transfer to the University of Illinois Urbana–Champaign do just as well academically, as reflected by graduating grade point average, as native students. The ease with which your students transfer from your college, and their success rates once they do, must be emphasized.

For the first time in College of DuPage's nearly 48-year history, our board of trustees decided recently to reduce tuition by $4 per credit for the spring 2015 semester. Yes—*reduce.* A reduction was not an easy decision, but it was one I was willing to support due to the college's sound fiscal situation. The average student will save approximately $60 for 15 credit hours this spring, but it's not just the dollars saved that matters. It's our willingness to put the student first that counts. This is a form of indirect marketing. We also have developed a Presidential Scholars program that rewards high achievement in high school by providing these students with a free education at College of DuPage. For the fall of 2014, the third year of this program, 362 applicants met the rigorous Presidential Scholarship criteria; we granted 130 scholarships, providing roughly $468,000. Academically enriched students attract academically enriched students, which reinforces our brand of quality. We have always provided opportunities for challenged students, academically or otherwise; here is where future enrollment growth can be found. We are on more radar screens for our academic excellence.

Another avenue to consider regarding price is differential tuition. At College of DuPage, we charge different tuition rates for select technical programs such as nursing, which is more expensive to provide, and we have seen no resistance or loss of enrollment.

Place: Don't be afraid to buy trees

The core business at any community college is teaching and learning. For the past 48 years, College of DuPage has offered students excellence through academics. However, it wasn't until recently that our outside finally matched the superior product we offer inside our walls. College of DuPage is on the cusp of finishing a complete overhaul of our campus through both new construction and renovation. Through two capital referenda in 2002 and 2010, we generated almost $400 million. Over five years, we have spent upward of $550 million to provide the finest teaching and learning space possible. No building is older than 2009, and we operate 2.4 million square feet of space. Selling the referenda offered a wonderful marketing opportunity to tell our story and base our request on the value we bring to the table. Our ability to do this stemmed from an excellent reputation in our community. We demonstrated to our taxpayers through a comprehensive, truthful and vivid campaign the value of our institution in order to garner their approval of this 12-year project. We continue to reap the benefits from that campaign.

Although you can't judge a book by its cover, it is my experience that students can and do judge a campus by its appearance. Within a matter of minutes of being on campus, they'll decide whether they want to attend your college. A crucial mistake I have seen many presidents make is not keeping their campuses visually pleasing. This means creating gathering spaces for students so that they want to stay on campus and enjoy their experience between classes. At College of DuPage, the beautification of our campus is taken very seriously, down to the smallest detail—from keeping trash off the ground to creating good landscaping to repairing cracked sidewalks and potholes. Do not be afraid to spend consequential dollars on landscaping. Do not be afraid to buy trees. You will take some criticism from those who do not understand the importance of your campus's physical appeal. However, as part of consistent beautification, good landscaping will pay for itself in enrollment.

Be vigilant and enlist all of your employees to help maintain your college. At College of DuPage, we started the campaign "Be a Hero, Call 4440" to encourage people to call physical facilities management if they see something in need of cleaning or repair. Similarly, at Harper College, we had the "Sharper Harper" campaign. At Harper, when we were invaded by geese, we hired border collies to clear them out. At Penn College, we removed abandoned railroad tracks, industrial smokestacks, pole-mounted early-20th-century power transformers and three condemned buildings. The list goes on. In my early years at Penn College, Harper College and College of DuPage, I was embarrassed to walk around campus. I did not feel I could look someone in the eye and say with confidence that we really are good at what we do. Make everyone feel responsible for their place of work, and you will be amazed by the results. At College of DuPage, we created "outside rooms" like waterfall hill, APEX, and our student-designed gazebo, for students to gather and, we hope, remain on campus longer, which garners obvious benefits. If you have one takeaway from my discussion of place, I hope it gives you the fortitude to spend the money to present a physical plant that tells your story.

Earlier I mentioned the importance of your products on the shelves, but note that products can be items other than academic programs. At Penn College (then known as

Williamsport Area Community College), we introduced a new "product" in the form of funding and building the Advanced Technology and Health Sciences Center, which now bears my name. We used the construction of this building to change how people talked about the college, which was hanging by a thread at the time due to loss of local sponsorship from 22 school districts that had traditionally paid one-third of the tuition of their residents. We created a conversation around this building about economic development in the region and the crucial role we should play in it. People began to see us as a potential game-changer for the region's economic health.

An emphasis on a good and interesting "Place" lends itself to getting nontraditional foot traffic on your campus, which can lead to more enrollment, potential donors or public support when it is time to go to the people with a referendum. At College of DuPage, we provide wonderful spaces for students to learn, but we also have created beautiful gathering places for students and community members to enjoy. For example, we have a fine-dining restaurant that serves as a learning opportunity for students, as well as an excellent location to host college and community events. Two days a week during the academic year, the restaurant is student run. The other five days it is professionally operated as a business rather than being allowed to sit idle. The restaurant brought 16,000 people to our campus in fiscal year 2014; even if it costs money, it is tremendous marketing for the college.

Among our many activities, we established a food and wine festival that has tripled in size in three years, with almost 600 people at the latest event. In the last year, the college's McAninch Arts Center hosted 144 musical, dance, theater and other programs that have drawn more than 47,000 people to our campus. We also spent $2 million to create our Lakeside Pavilion, located next to the Arts Center. The Chicago area has a famous outdoor venue called Ravinia. I like to think of our Lakeside Pavilion as "Ravinia West." During the pavilion's first summer, nearly 7,800 individuals attended our free inaugural Lakeside Pavilion Summer Concert and Movie series. We also house the only jazz radio station in the Chicago area. Every component of our campus plays an important role at College of DuPage. Waterleaf, WDCB 90.9fm and the McAninch Arts Center connect people to us in ways that otherwise would not happen. We want people on campus, and we will get a return on investment from this exposure.

These physical features differentiate us from the competition—a vital concept in today's market. When I arrived at Harper College, most of our buildings reflected a 1960s or 1970s campus. Then we built the 285,000 square foot Avanté Center for Science, Health Careers and Emerging Technology, which represented our dedication to advancement and providing premier educational space for our students. Avanté provided an entirely different, 21st-century curb appeal. At Penn College, where I served as president for 17 years, we had the Lumley Aviation Center. Anyone flying into Williamsport had to taxi by this uniquely designed facility which, when seen from the air, was shaped like an airplane wing. We also acquired the Capitol Theatre in center-city Williamsport and elegantly restored it, creating the Williamsport Community Arts Center. This entailed multiple risks, including whether we would be able to raise the $11 million needed to renovate the facility (we were successful) and whether we could then operate the theater in a way that would pay for itself. I'm happy to say this gorgeous theater is today considered "the gem of Williamsport" and has operated in the black for more than 20 years. In its own way, it too shaped people's opinions of Penn College. At College of DuPage, we have declared first-responder training as a marquee program to set us apart from the competition. We constructed a $30 million Homeland Security Education Center with a complete indoor street scene for live simulations, forensics labs, a cyber-lab and a mock court room. We currently have under construction a $17 million Homeland Security Training Center that will contain a firing range and a virtual reality simulation lab. At times it seems we have more police on campus than students—a nice side benefit.

The argument that creating nontraditional facilities to attract students and community members to campus dilutes resources is just not true. These nontraditional attractions can be the reason people choose to attend a particular college. Get people on campus. If you can get people on campus, they will more likely want to be engaged and be a supporter. The parents, grandparents, friends or neighbors who communicate their positive experiences at your school offer more powerful advertising than any billboard or television ad. And let's not forget that you need to make it easy for people to find their way around your campus. It is well worth the investment to ensure way-finding through well-planned signage. Remember, make it easy for people to identify and use your facilities and services.

Within your "Place," you of course have students, many of whom are hard at work on projects that can be leveraged to market your institution. For example, College of DuPage architecture students this year added their own touch to our campus by providing an outdoor gathering pavilion. This beautiful wooden structure now resides next to our Technical Education Center, where it can easily be seen by passing traffic. At Penn College, we enthusiastically promoted student work on our campus—from design and construction of buildings like the Victorian House, the Professional Development Center, and the Morgan Valley Retreat—to the culinary/hospitality work in Le Jeune Chef. We used these student projects to reach new audiences in the general public, and the results continue to "wow" visitors to this day.

Promotion: Yell it from the mountaintops

The statement "if you build it, they will come" no longer applies to colleges. You have to provide *reasons* for prospective students, their parents and community members to visit your college. Whether for advising sessions, for a college fair or to visit an exceptional program or facility, marketing and promotion is essential to getting students to step foot on your campus. You can provide a Garden of Eden, but if people don't know about it, they won't make the effort to see your school. You must promote your college by involving and engaging people who will bring others.

To successfully market your institution, you must first find out how your community perceives you. While I was at Harper, we commissioned the college's first comprehensive awareness and preference survey. We learned that, although residents were highly aware of the college, they had no consistent, compelling impression of who we were or why we were relevant to them. These findings laid the groundwork for Harper's first institutional branding campaign while subsequent community surveys tracked our progress. We did the same thing at College of DuPage, conducting a scientific, quantitative survey of the public in 2010 prior to our last referendum. In preparation for the college's extensive re-branding process, we went to our constituents again in 2013 to conduct both quantitative and qualitative research through which we learned, among other things, that our district residents believe we provide a high-quality academic experience and diverse course offerings but were unaware of the student opportunities that provide an experience similar to four-year colleges.

Regarding the importance of the quality and creativity of your advertising, consider this: In a recent *Inside Higher Ed* article, Ellis Verdi, the owner of DeVito/Verdi, the Manhattan-based ad agency, said, "If your advertising looks institutional and boring, I would tell a student that's fair warning about the school. The advertising in and of itself is a presentation of who you are. It should be provocative, it should be smart, it should be witty." Your advertising and promotion, like your physical plant, will be taken as a reflection of who you are. You must be prepared to make an investment to ensure you are shown in the best possible light. I will not presume to design a detailed advertising plan for your institution. We all reside in unique media markets with varying levels of competition and resources at our disposal. In general, though, my own teams have shied away from television as too expensive to be effective, relying instead on radio; some print newspaper advertising (although less and less; display advertising is also very expensive and may not produce the needed return on investment, particularly as the role of traditional print newspapers continues to dwindle); an increased social media presence, including Facebook, Twitter, YouTube, a College of DuPage–specific student app and our IntelliResponse web service; and a great deal of direct marketing in the form of mailings and emails. You should also ensure that your promotion plan is in line with your institution's overall strategic plan. You would not want to make an investment in something that does not work in tandem with your college's intended direction. And make sure you have an updated style guide or standards manual that everyone adheres to when presenting your college to the community.

Promotion is not simply advertising. There are other ideas to consider. There is "thought leadership" through authoring and placing articles in external regional venues. Ensure that your relationships with the local press are good; take the time to meet personally with, and have an occasional breakfast or lunch with, editors. Does your communications team have mechanisms to regularly tout your accomplished faculty and students? At College of DuPage we have faculty and student spotlights on our website, highlighting key individuals. Does your institution have a speakers bureau to send out your faculty experts to speak at local Rotary clubs, chambers of commerce, libraries and seniors groups? At College of DuPage we started COD Cares, a volunteer corps of college employees and students who regularly go into the community to perform good works. Do you have active representation at your local chamber of commerce? If you have the facility, have you considered offering it as a venue to your chamber or other community groups?

Another marketing tactic is to host major events on your campus. The College of DuPage Homeland Security Education Center served as the command center for various government security agencies during the 2012 NATO summit in Chicago. This gave us excellent exposure with potential future training partners. We also host paid webinars for emergency responders throughout the state and beyond, further making our presence known on a national level. At Penn College, we held an annual Spring Open House for the community in which every academic department had a major activity, drawing more than 1,000 community members to our campus on a Sunday in March when community members sought activity.

If you have the technology in house or a friendly local-access cable channel, consider taking your college into the living rooms of your district residents. During my presidency at Penn College, we launched the award-winning television series called *Penn College and You.* It began in 1995 as a 60-minute, studio-based call-in show, produced in cooperation with our local cable television station. The program evolved over the years, and it is now a 30-minute, career-awareness documentary series that runs on public television—now called *Degrees That Work.* In the beginning, we featured campus experts speaking on issues important to the community. An early episode featured our best-known culinary professor. It was so well received that we decided to build another television series called *You're the Chef,* which had a long and successful run.

There is a gold standard brand of hunting calls known as Primos. Their tagline has always resonated with me: "Speak the Language." That is what you have to do with your community members and prospective students, who are different ages, ethnicities and backgrounds. As I hope your marketing team will tell you, to some degree you must "segment" your messaging to make sure you are speaking to as much of your community as possible. Your advertising materials should be colorful, active and, when possible, original in their conception. As an example, my institution no longer publishes a traditional annual report. (I've never believed the average person cares about the typical annual report; by its nature it is numbers heavy, story light and incredibly boring.) Instead we developed a community-wide news magazine released three times a year called *IMPACT,* which is delivered to the 390,000 households of our district. As the name might suggest, this award-winning publication is devoted to showing the community the impact we have had in our residents' lives, highlighting programs and people at the college who are making a difference. At Penn College, we published *One College Avenue,* and it also told our story in interesting and engaging pieces that promoted the institution. Not only does it inform our tax base of what their community college is doing, but also it provides a strong visual advertisement.

At Penn College, we had the tagline "Pennsylvania's Premier Technical College." While it's not very sexy, the descriptive line worked—so much so that even the former governor of Pennsylvania used the phrase when discussing the school. At Harper College, our "Go Forward" tagline was also very effective, as it pushed action on the students and implied the school would offer a helping hand. At College of DuPage, we are known for the "Value of a Lifetime," which has meaning on many different levels for students. In addition, this past year, we elevated this messaging through our recent branding campaign, "Welcome to the New School of Thought." This statement creates a feeling among students that they are part of something bigger than just completing so many credits to earn a degree or certificate to transfer or enter the workforce. This new branding campaign—which emanates through everything we produce in our marketing department—reinforces to students that College of DuPage's value extends beyond pricing. They are part of something bigger that speaks to their achievement both academically and as people who will make a solid, tangible contribution, wherever their paths lead. I would stress that branding is much more than creating a new tagline. We spent roughly $300,000 with an outside national firm to perform several months of detailed, intensive research leading up to a complex, nuanced new way to tell our story. This is serious money, but you have to be willing to spend on your image. It is an investment, and if you don't grow in enrollment, it sends a bad message and you lose revenue, which we all need as states fail to shoulder their fiscal responsibility.

Promotion cannot occur effectively without the first four "Ps," and it is not a discreet set of functions such as placing ads or sending out news releases. This "support and active encouragement" to attend your college is accomplished through both overt, traditional methods (advertising, news releases, catalogs, brochures) and more indirect means (word of mouth, non-education-related events, creating relationships within the community).

You have to do more than keep the lights on

In today's competitive environment, it's not enough to hang a shingle and put an "open" sign out front; you must aggressively go after market share. The bottom line is that marketing facilitates the achievement of outcomes. If you want to grow your business, you must invest in telling your story. You must distinguish and differentiate yourself from the competition. If you want to run with the big dogs, you must look and act and play like the big dogs.

Unfortunately—even today, when community colleges have the support and esteem of the president of the United States—much of our promotion must be used to debunk the stigma associated with attending a community college and debunk the idea that we are somehow less than our four-year peers. Effective marketing neutralizes critics, naysayers and people who don't have an informed idea about the mission of community colleges.

Some interesting recent facts released by Sally Mae and discussed in the *Chronicle of Higher Education*: More than 7 million students are attending community college in the United States at any given time. According to the American Association of Community Colleges 2014 Fact Sheet, enrollment at two-year colleges comprises 45 percent of all higher-education students in the United States. That more families are turning to two-year colleges is perhaps the most telling. Truly this is our time to capitalize on changing attitudes.

A few other items I'd like to note:

Enrollment matters. Beyond the additional revenue, growing enrollment demonstrates the institution's vitality, which I believe attracts people. Success breeds success. In the spring of 2014, College of DuPage was the only community college district in Illinois to increase enrollment. If you don't increase enrollment, people are likely to ask, "What's wrong?" College of DuPage is seeing increases in traditional students, out-of-district students and international students. Did we sit back modestly when we achieved this enrollment success? Heck, no! We trumpeted it from the rooftops both internally and in the media. We immediately asked, "How can we capitalize on this good news to further grow our business?" Between fall 2013 and fall 2014, no other Illinois community college district added more headcount than College of DuPage, which increased by 3 percent.

Do not underestimate the marketing benefit you will receive from special programs. At Harper and now College of DuPage, we have summer bridge programs designed to give incoming freshmen a head start and to help with the transition to college. We had the Black Teen Summit at Harper, which gathered a panel of successful black professionals who could share their experiences with teens from the region's high schools. Important for our marketing efforts, it also gave students a chance to meet our counselors and see our facilities. At College of DuPage, we offer a dual credit program that exposes high school students to the college. We have the Pathways to Engineering program, which provides a seamless transition for our engineering students to transfer to the University of Illinois Engineering program after two years with us. The college also has Business Solutions, which offers affordable on-site training designed to meet specific business needs, as well as the Suburban Law Enforcement Academy, which trains thousands of Illinois law enforcement officers.

Internally, we also have Enhance COD, in which employees are encouraged to submit ideas monthly to improve the college; Centers for Excellence, which is a special designation and funding given to select academic programs that meet rigorous criteria; and our Idea Center, which is a campus hub for innovation in teaching, learning and student success. By engaging these programs, we create new marketing opportunities for ourselves. If you have people with new ideas, you can use that to grow and tap into new markets. Then you have yet another way to tell your story.

Fundraising is another area that deserves your attention. Although the primary function of your foundation is to raise dollars for the institution, its other function is to cultivate friends and build lasting relationships. The successful people who ultimately give to your college or sit on your foundation board are ambassadors telling your story. Philanthropy is a real means by which we influence people and market ourselves. When you ask for a donation, you are obliged to have a good story to tell.

I mentioned earlier running with the big dogs. Universities are very attached to their mascots. They play strongly to their athletic and spirit colors. They make their students walking billboards. That's why at College of DuPage we, along with our student body, recently invested the funds in an eight-foot bronze chaparral (also known as a road-runner). Within the year, it became the spot on campus for students and their families to have their pictures taken. Speaking of athletics, they too can differentiate you from the competition. College of DuPage is home to the only community college football team in the state of Illinois, and we are celebrating this fall the college's first homecoming week in approximately 40 years. At Penn College, we started a nationally recognized archery team. Unique sports can set you apart.

There are two more "Ps" I'd like to highlight in terms of effective marketing. The sixth "P" is Persistence. Marketing is not a one-time activity; it is a full-time commitment that must be constant and consistent. Marketing requires a continuous flood of messaging; a one-time cloudburst of activity will quickly be forgotten.

The final "P" is Pride. It's no longer only about price at community colleges, or the people with whom students meet and interact, the classes they complete and the facilities that house the institution's product. Students who feel proud of their college, their education and their experience are more important to us out in the marketplace than any campaign we develop. They tell the true tale of a college's success. A nice bit of anecdotal evidence to monitor at your institution is how well your bookstore is selling its spirit wear. In the past few years, we have seen a significant increase in the number of College of DuPage sweatshirts, T-shirts, hats, and the like being worn around the college. Students are proud of their school and want others to know where they are reaching their higher education goals.

It's been my observation that education follows the corporate world by about 20 years. I believe we will see higher education institutions go out of business, and mergers will become more commonplace—first in the private sector and then in the public sector, as state funding dwindles and we are forced to depend less on the state and stand on our own. Colleges that do not grow, that do not differentiate themselves from the competition, that do not project a strong academic reputation and that do not look the part will place themselves at risk.

And finally, a strong balance sheet means you will have opportunities. The secret is to spend where there is the best return on investment. Do not shortchange your marketing efforts. If you do, you will eventually attenuate your college's position in the market-place. More than ever before, we must take control of our future, lest others define it for us. An aggressive, comprehensive marketing effort from the inside out is one arrow you must have in your quiver to ensure future success.

***

My thanks to College of DuPage Vice President for Marketing and Communications Joe Moore and Manager of Media Relations Robyn Johnson for their assistance with this chapter. Thanks also to Mike Barzacchini, director of marketing services, William Rainey Harper College; and Elaine Lambert, special assistant to the president for creative development and public relations, Pennsylvania College of Technology, for their contributions.

ABOUT THE AUTHORS

Bryan D. Albrecht, Ed.D., serves as the president and chief executive officer of Gateway Technical College. Gateway is located in southeastern Wisconsin and serves approximately 25,000 students annually. Gateway is known for having strong partnerships with the business community and for establishing a culture of innovation. Under Albrecht's leadership, Gateway has expanded programs and services, built a national industry training network and enhanced the talent pipeline from high school through postgraduate-level studies. Albrecht serves on the Southeast Wisconsin Workforce Development Board, as well as national boards including the Manufacturing Institute, the National Occupational Competency Testing Institute, the STEM Academy, and the Center for Occupational Research and Development. His experience has led him to testify before the U.S. Congress on career and technical education issues, as well as being named a distinguished educator by the International Technology and Engineering Educators Association. Albrecht earned his bachelor's, master's and education specialist degrees from the University of Wisconsin–Stout and his doctorate of education from the University of Minnesota.

Robert L. Breuder, Ph.D., is the fifth president of College of DuPage, which in the fall of 2014 served more than 29,000 students and is the second largest provider of undergraduate education in Illinois. Raised in Queens, New York, Breuder earned his doctorate in higher education administration from Florida State University in 1972 and began his career as an instructor of botany at Paul Smith's College in New York. In 1981 at the age of 36, Breuder became the youngest community college president in the nation at Pennsylvania College of Technology (formerly Williamsport Area Community College) in Williamsport, Penn. Prior to arriving at College of DuPage in January 2009, Breuder was president of William Rainey Harper College in Palatine, Ill., where he had served since 1998.

Linnie S. Carter, Ph.D., APR, is the vice president of college advancement at HACC, Central Pennsylvania's Community College, and the executive director of the HACC

Foundation. She oversees many functions, including alumni affairs, fundraising, grants, integrated marketing communications and web development. She previously led the advancement offices and foundations at two community colleges in Virginia and one community college in North Carolina. In addition, she served two four-year institutions—one in Virginia and one in North Carolina—as an advancement professional and professor, respectively. Carter has 22 years of advancement experience and earned a doctorate in community college leadership from Old Dominion University. She also has bachelor's and master's degrees in mass communications from Virginia Commonwealth University.

Thom D. Chesney, Ph.D., was named president of Brookhaven College in August 2011. His circuitous pathway to the chief fundraiser role includes academic posts at the University of Texas at Dallas, Collin County Community College (Texas), Pennsylvania College of Technology, Texas Wesleyan University and Whitman College (Wash.). He earned his doctorate in English literature from Florida State University, completing a dissertation on George Orwell; a master's degree in creative writing from Minnesota State University, Mankato; and a bachelor's degree in Spanish from Washington University in St. Louis. Running concurrent with his appointments in academe are decades of volunteer service on chambers of commerce, nonprofit boards, commissions and election campaigns; jobs in retail sales, manufacturing and service industries; and contribution of his voice and writing talent to stage, television and radio. He begins nearly every workday writing by hand a variety of cards, letters and other personal correspondence, which frames the day ahead for building and sustaining relationships and opportunities.

Catherine Chew, Ed.D., became the fourth president and first female leader of Craven Community College in 2008. A progressive career track in higher education, including positions in the university environment and dynamic community colleges in the Northeast, South and Midwest, has given her a breadth of knowledge and experience. While at the University of Wisconsin–Madison, she wrote two best-seller resource guides on career pathways, and in 2012 she was selected as a Fulbright Scholar in Germany. Throughout her career, Chew has been a strong advocate of students, an avid promoter of partnerships and fundraising, and a devotee of professional development and globalization. Deeply committed to the mission and philosophy of the community college, Chew recognizes these institutions are one of the nation's most valuable assets. As president and as servant leader, she is committed to serving students, colleagues and the community. She believes, as the late world human rights leader Nelson Mandela did, "Education is the most powerful weapon which you can use to change the world."

Carol A. Churchill has worked in community college administration for more than 26 years. She was the fifth president of Mid Michigan Community College (MMCC), where she served until her retirement in 2014. Under her leadership, MMCC experienced unparalleled growth and embarked on an ambitious campus expansion and renovation plan supported by the college's first capital campaign. While at MMCC, Churchill was known for engaging stakeholders in strategic planning, for her active involvement in the many communities served by the college and for her tenacity in developing alternative funding sources. Prior to MMCC, Churchill held the positions of dean of student success and vice provost for economic and workforce development at Macomb Community College. Her 15-year career at Southwestern Michigan College culminated in the position of vice president for student services. Churchill earned an associate degree from Southwestern Michigan College and bachelor's and master's degrees from Western Michigan University. She and her husband, Jim, operated a family farm for more than 25 years. They have three children and eight grandchildren.

William R. Crowe, MBA, Ph.D., is a senior public service faculty member at the University of Georgia, with a research interest in community college advancement, leadership and capacity building. Prior to coming to Georgia, Crowe spent 25 years at Tyler Junior College in Texas, the last 15 years as president. During Crowe's presidency at Tyler, the institution built a strong advancement operation to support the college. That organization included a vibrant alumni association, a strong development team and significant growth in both annual giving and endowed funds. Tyler Junior College currently has the sixth largest community college support foundation in the country and is consistently one of the top annual fundraisers among U.S. community colleges. The unique combination of experience and research gives Crowe valuable insights into the world of advancement in today's community colleges. Crowe holds an undergraduate degree in business from the University of Texas at Austin and an MBA and is a distinguished graduate of the Community College Leadership Program at the University of Texas at Austin.

Charlene Mickens Dukes, Ed.D., is the eighth and first female president of Prince George's Community College (PGCC). She holds membership in a variety of professional organizations, including the boards of directors of the American Association of Community Colleges, the American Association of Colleges and Universities, the Community College Advisory Panel of the College Board, the Institute for Higher Education Policy, the Presidents' RoundTable and the National Council on Black American Affairs. Dukes is a member of the board of directors of the Prince George's County Chamber of Commerce, the Business Round Table, Doctors' Community Hospital, College Summit of the National Capital Region, and Hillside-Works Scholarship Connection. She is on the board of directors of the Harlem Renaissance Foundation and the Community Foundation of the National Capital Area. She serves as secretary of the Presidents' Round Table and co-coordinated the Thomas Lakin Institute for Mentored Leadership from 2009 to the present. She is currently the president of the Maryland State Board of Education. She holds a bachelor's degree from Indiana University of Pennsylvania, and a master's and a doctorate in administrative and policy studies from the University of Pittsburgh.

Rufus Glasper, Ph.D., CPA, is the chancellor of the Maricopa County Community College District, one of the nation's largest systems of community colleges. As CEO, Glasper has paved the education and training pathway for students to receive career training, to transfer to a baccalaureate-granting institution, or to take personal interest courses for individual growth and development. Glasper's leadership is built on three pillars: student success, public stewardship and "ONE Maricopa." Glasper is a staunch advocate for educational access and opportunity and has established inclusiveness, engagement and respect as the guiding principles of his administration. He serves as a leader of a statewide effort shaping the future of higher education in Arizona and is a member of numerous boards and organizations whose purposes are to improve higher education locally, nationally and internationally. Glasper earned a bachelor's degree from Luther College, a master's and advanced degrees from Northern Illinois University, and a doctorate in higher education finance from the University of Arizona.

Rae Goldsmith is the chief marketing and communications officer at Southern Illinois University (SIU). She joined SIU in August 2013, after serving for more than eight years as a vice president for CASE, where she led the development and delivery of advancement content through the offices of communications, books publishing, CURRENTS magazine, the CASE InfoCenter and research. She joined the CASE staff after more than 20 years leading communications and marketing initiatives at the University of Louisville, Central Michigan University and Ball State University, where she earned bachelor's and master's degrees. An active CASE volunteer, Goldsmith has chaired the Annual Assembly (now the Summit for Leaders in Advancement) and the Conference for Senior Public Relations Professionals, served on the Commission on Communications and Marketing and the District III board, and been a frequent CURRENTS author and conference speaker. She is an eight-year veteran of the Summer Institute faculty and has been recognized with the CASE Crystal Apple Award for outstanding teaching at CASE conferences.

Carrie Besnette Hauser, Ph.D., is president and CEO of Colorado Mountain College, which has seven campuses and 11 learning locations serving 12,000 square miles of the central Rocky Mountains. Previously, she has been a senior executive at the Ewing Marion Kauffman Foundation, Metropolitan State University of Denver and the Daniels Fund. Her teaching background includes assignments at UCLA, the University of Denver and Colorado State University. She has served on the staffs of the Western Interstate Commission for Higher Education and the University of Arizona, her undergraduate alma mater. She earned her master's and doctorate degrees from UCLA and is a graduate of the Wharton School of Business. At the national level, Hauser is past president of the National Scholarship Providers Association (NSPA) and has served on the Pathways to College Network executive committee and as an Educational Policy Institute board member. An avid outdoorswoman, Hauser has summited Mt. Kilimanjaro (raising funds for the NSPA), climbed to the Mt. Everest base camp and was a Grand Canyon river guide. She and her husband enjoy skiing, backpacking, biking and exploring the Rocky Mountain West and remote places around the world.

Paul C. Heaton was named the inaugural director of the CASE Center for Community College Advancement in May 2011. He joined CASE after five years at Northwestern Michigan College, a community college in Traverse City, Michigan, where he was responsible for public relations, marketing and communications, as well as the school's public radio station. He also supported the college's fundraising efforts, which earned a CASE-WealthEngine award for overall performance in 2007. In addition to his work at a community college, Paul has held leadership positions in marketing, communications, public relations and student media at Eastern Michigan University and the Interlochen Center for the Arts in Michigan and at Ithaca College in New York. Prior to working in higher education, he was an editor and bureau chief for the *St. Petersburg Times* in Florida. He has a bachelor's degree in journalism and political science from Indiana University and a master's degree in communications from Ithaca College.

Lee D. Lambert, J.D., has been chancellor of Pima Community College since 2013. Before coming to Pima, he was president of Shoreline Community College in Washington, where he also served as interim president and vice president for human resources and legal affairs. Before Shoreline, Lambert was vice president for human resources and legal affairs at Centralia College in Washington, and special assistant to the president for civil rights and legal affairs at Evergreen State College in Washington. Lambert served on the 2013–14 Executive Committee of the American Association of Community Colleges (AACC), and he chairs the AACC's Committee on Program Initiatives and Workforce Training. He received the Pacific Region 2009 Chief Executive Officer Award from the Association of Community College Trustees. Lambert received a juris doctor degree from the Seattle University School of Law and a bachelor's degree in liberal arts from Evergreen State College in Olympia, Wash. A U.S. Army veteran, Lambert was born in South Korea, grew up on three continents and graduated from high school in the Olympia area.

E. Ann McGee, Ed.D., was selected as president of Seminole State College of Florida in 1996. McGee is a graduate of St. Petersburg College, Florida State University (FSU) and Nova Southeastern University. She was named Most Outstanding Graduate at SPC and Phi Beta Kappa at FSU and was inducted into the Practitioner's Hall of Fame at Nova. Governor Bush appointed her as a charter trustee at FSU. McGee began her career teaching speech and English and then served as dean of student services at Florida Keys Community College. Her next position was campus provost at Broward College in Florida. For the 10 years prior to Seminole, she was vice president for development and executive director of the Foundation for Broward College. McGee currently serves on the American

Association of Community Colleges (AACC) board, the Phi Theta Kappa Foundation, the Foundation for the Florida College System, and other local philanthropic and economic development boards. She is the immediate past chair of AACC's President's Academy and served two terms on the CASE Board of Trustees.

Brenda S. Mitchell is the executive director of the Office of Institutional Advancement and Foundation at Prince George's Community College (PGCC) in Largo, Maryland. With 25 years of progressive experience in the nonprofit sector and in fundraising, she has invaluable insight in most resource development functions, including strategic planning, capital campaigns, major gifts, annual giving, alumni relations, special events, communication and marketing, foundation board relations, sponsored programs and grants. Under Mitchell's leadership, PGCC is served by an integrated grants and resource development office, housed under the Office of Institutional Advancement, which raises both public and private funds for the college, leading efforts to build mutually beneficial partnerships and leverage resources with the public, private and nonprofit sectors. She is a board member of CASE District II, the Council for Resource Development (regional director, 2008–2010), the Association of Fundraising Professionals, Leadership Prince George's and the Maryland Association of Nonprofit Organizations. She received a bachelor's degree from Virginia Commonwealth University and a master's degree from the University of Maryland University College.

DeRionne P. Pollard, Ph.D., is president of Montgomery College, one of the largest undergraduate institutions in Maryland, serving nearly 60,000 credit and noncredit students annually at its three campuses. Since arriving in 2010, she has spearheaded the development of a new Montgomery College mission and Montgomery College 2020, the institution's strategic plan. She recently served on the American Association of Community Colleges' 21st-Century Commission on the Future of Community Colleges. Currently, Pollard is a member of the Community College Advisory Panel at the College Board and the Higher Education Research and Development Institute Advisory Board. She serves on several regional boards, including the Montgomery County Business Development Corporation, the Montgomery County Chamber of Commerce, the Tech Council of Maryland and Generation Hope. Pollard also graduated from the Leadership Montgomery program and was named its Outstanding Leader for 2013. She formerly served as president of Las Positas College in California and as an English instructor at College of Lake County in Illinois. She received her doctorate from Loyola University and her bachelor's and master's degrees from Iowa State University.

Robert H. Sandel, Ed.D., has been president of Virginia Western Community College for 13 years and is a driving force behind ensuring that the college is accessible and affordable and that its students are achieving success. He also has overseen extensive new construction, renovations and upgrades to campus. A native of Orangeburg, S.C.,

Sandel is a Roanoker at heart. He has been actively involved in the community, serving on numerous local and state boards, including the Roanoke Regional Chamber of Commerce, Smart Beginnings and the LewisGale Medical Center. He has served as the chair for the VCCS Achieve 2015 Strategic Planning process for the entire 23-college system. Sandel earned his bachelor's degree from The Citadel, his master's degree from South Carolina State University and his doctorate from the University of South Carolina. Prior to joining Virginia Western, he was president of Mountain Empire Community College and has been a community college educator for more than 30 years. Sandel's wife, Jane, recently retired from high school teaching. They have four children and 10 grandchildren.

Paul Schwalbach has worked as a writer in Pima Community College's Office of Communications and Marketing since April 2009. Previously, he was a writer and editor at the *Tucson* (Ariz.) *Citizen* newspaper. He has a bachelor's degree in political science from the University of Arizona and is working toward an associate degree in paralegal studies at Pima Community College.

William T. Scroggins, Ph.D., became Mt. San Antonio College's ninth president in 2011. Under his guidance, the Mt. SAC Foundation has brought in new leadership, reinvigorated the board, restructured finances, engaged new donors, and funded operational and academic projects. Scroggins has amassed 39 years of experience in education—26 of those as a chemistry professor and 13 as an administrator. Prior to coming to Mt. SAC, he served as president of College of the Sequoias. Under Scroggins's leadership, the college passed three bond measures, creating two new campuses. The foundation oversaw funding of these bond measures, reached out to a much broader donor base and established a major gift program that increased the unrestricted endowment 10-fold to $6 million. Scroggins has a bachelor's degree in chemistry from UCLA and a doctorate in chemistry from University of California–Riverside. During his teaching career, he served in a number of leadership positions, culminating in a two-year term as president of the state Academic Senate.

David M. Sears joined Montgomery College in 2005 as the vice president of institutional advancement. During that time he led a successful capital campaign for the Montgomery College Foundation, which raised $25 million. In 2012 he was promoted to senior vice president for advancement and community engagement, supervising departments including development, alumni relations, marketing, communications, creative services, special events, grants, foundation finance and community engagement. In addition, he oversees the Life Sciences Park Foundation in Germantown and the Montgomery College Foundation. Prior to his arrival at Montgomery College, he worked as the director of athletic development at Georgetown University, where he raised $54 million for athletic scholarships, programs and facilities. He has also served as the vice president for advancement for Loyola University Maryland. Sears is an active member of the CASE

Center for Community College Advancement Advisory Committee and a former board member for Interfaith Works in Montgomery County. He earned his bachelor's degree from Georgetown University, his MBA from Mount St. Mary's University, and is actively pursuing his doctoral degree from the University of Maryland, Baltimore County.

Mick Starcevich, Ed.D., assumed the Kirkwood Community College presidency in 2005, having served previously as executive vice president at the college. He earned bachelor's and master's degrees from the University of Northern Iowa and a doctoral degree from Drake University. Starcevich has taught mathematics and served as assistant principal, principal and superintendent in Iowa schools for more than 30 years. Prior to coming to Kirkwood, he served as superintendent at College Community School District in Cedar Rapids, Iowa, for 11 years. He also served as an adjunct professor at Drake University for 20 years. He currently serves on a variety of community, state and national boards, including Junior Achievement, US Bank, Horizon's Family Services, Iowa Community College Presidents, Community Colleges for International Development, Community College Humanities Association and the League for Innovation in the Community College. He and his wife, Linda, have been married for 46 years and have two children and one grandchild.

Karen A. Stout, Ed.D., is president of Montgomery County Community College, a multicampus college in suburban Philadelphia. Stout moved into the presidency along a nontraditional pathway that included founding one community college foundation early in her career and serving as the chief development officer at three community colleges, along with an array of responsibilities in student affairs, information technology, marketing and research, strategic planning and campus leadership, before moving into the presidency at Montgomery in 2001. In her 14 years at Montgomery, Stout has placed student success and building the college's advancement and entrepreneurial capacity to support students at the heart of her leadership agenda. In 2014 the college earned the prestigious Leah Meyer Austin award from Achieving the Dream for its work around equity and student success and is a recognized national leader in the use of technology and analytics to improve teaching and learning. In February 2015 she was named president and CEO of Achieving the Dream, effective July 1, 2015.

John J. "Ski" Sygielski, Ed.D., became the seventh president of HACC, Central Pennsylvania's Community College, in 2011. His previous appointments include president of Mt. Hood Community College in Oregon, president of Lord Fairfax Community College in Virginia, and first vice chancellor for workforce and economic development of the Virginia Community College System. He has a bachelor's degree in philosophy, two master's degrees and a doctorate.

INDEX

D

E

F

G

H

I

J

K

L

M

N

O

P

ABOUT CASE

The Council for Advancement and Support of Education (CASE) is a professional association serving educational institutions and the advancement professionals who work on their behalf in alumni relations, communications, development, marketing and allied areas.

Founded in 1974, CASE maintains headquarters in Washington, D.C., with offices in London, Singapore, and Mexico City. Its membership includes more than 3,600 colleges and universities, primary and secondary independent and international schools, and nonprofit organizations in nearly 80 countries. CASE serves more than 77,000 advancement professionals on the staffs of its member institutions and has more than 17,000 professional members on its roster.

CASE also offers a variety of advancement products and services, provides standards and an ethical framework for the profession, and works with other organizations to respond to public issues of concern while promoting the importance of education worldwide.